D0868013

Ezekiel

· · ·

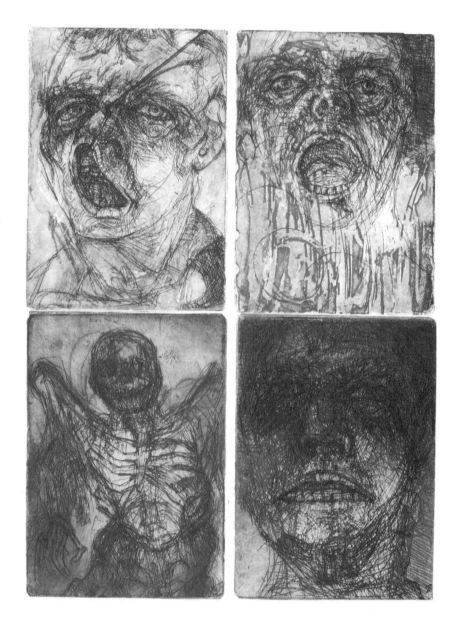

Ezekiel

Vision in the Dust

• • •

Daniel Berrigan

with art by
Tom Lewis-Borbely

ORBIS BOOKS

Maryknoll, New York 10545

Dedicated to the Prince of Peace Plowshares
and their biblical witness

Philip Berrigan, Mark Colville, Steve Baggarly
Susan Crane, Stephen Kelly, S.J., Tom Lewis-Borbely

The Catholic Foreign Mission Society of America (Maryknoll) recruits and trains people for overseas missionary service. Through Orbis Books, Maryknoll aims to foster the international dialogue that is essential to mission. The books published, however, reflect the opinions of their authors and are not meant to represent the official position of the society.

Copyright © 1997 Daniel Berrigan

Art copyright © 1997 by Tom Lewis-Borbely

Published by Orbis Books, Maryknoll, New York, U.S.A.

All rights reserved. No part of this publication may be reproduced or transmitted in any form or by any means, electronic or mechanical, including photocopying, recording, or any information storage or retrieval system, without prior permission in writing from the publisher. For permissions write to Orbis Books, P.O. Box 308, Maryknoll, NY 10545-0308, U.S.A.

Manufactured in the United States of America

Library of Congress Cataloging-in-Publication Data
Berrigan, Daniel.
    Ezekiel : vision in the dust / Daniel Berrigan : with art by Tom
Lewis-Borbely.
        p. cm.
    ISBN 1-57075-135-8 (alk. paper)
    1. Bible. O.T. Ezekiel – Meditations. I. Title.
BS1545.4.B47 1997
224'.406 – dc21   97-24654
                                                       CIP

Contents

Artist's Introduction

In the spring of 1994 I went to a retreat on the Book of Ezekiel at Kirkridge, Pennsylvania, led by Daniel Berrigan. Dan worked from his manuscript of this book, from poetry, and from the Bible, leading us in the tradition of all great teachers to teach ourselves. It was during this weekend retreat that I decided to start an etching series on the Book of Ezekiel. Dan was very supportive and allowed me to make a photocopy of his working manuscript and poems. My work began that weekend and continued for two years, using Dan's work and the Ezekiel text from the Bible. This became an artistic journey that would deepen my understanding of the biblical text and images and bring me to understand the present through Ezekiel's vision. Searching for a technical solution, I also discovered a very new printmaking technique of nontoxic photo-etching.

I am no stranger to Dan Berrigan's prose and poetry. My first real encounter began in the Baltimore County Jail, where Dan and I were imprisoned together after the Catonsville Nine protest in 1968. One of the results of our jail-time was the artwork for Dan's book *Trial Poems.* Reflecting on that time in jail, I wrote: "I have always believed that an artist is an artist, in jail or out of jail. So there I was in my studio, a four by six cell. My art materials were limited. I managed to get a few sheets of sketch paper, a small bottle of india ink; but there was not enough black for the poems, so I added a mixture of ground cigarette ashes and water. For the brown background I mixed a combination of instant coffee and cocoa. Finally I shaped a few Popsicle sticks into pens." I worked with Dan on two other published collaborations: *Vietnamese Letter,* in the mid-1970s, and *The Nightmare of God,* which was written in the 1980s and is based on the Book of Revelation. For the latter I created twelve eighteen-inch by twenty-four-inch photo-etchings. But, like many other artists, I had to stop using the technique in the 1980s, when our awareness developed of the toxic hazards of this printmaking method.

My commitment at the 1994 retreat in Pennsylvania to begin and complete the Ezekiel series included a commitment to chemically safe and nontoxic etching techniques. I was given invaluable help by Keith Howard, director of the Canadian School for Non-toxic Printmaking at Grande Prairie Regional College in Alberta, Canada. Keith's present and past work justifies his designation as the father of nontoxic photo-etching. For my etching plate I chose roofing copper because of its low cost and availability at many hardware stores. I started with twenty-five plates and went through almost three hundred before I was finished. I also taught two nontoxic photo-etching workshops at the Worcester Art Museum, during which time I continued the technical exploration with my printmaking students.

My study of the Bible continued with additional retreats at Kirkridge led by Dan on Isaiah, Jeremiah, and the New Testament. At these sessions I always exhibited the in-progress Ezekiel Series, which was progressing and deepening in its perspective. I sketched images in soup kitchens, on buses, at demonstrations at the Pentagon, and in the quiet woods of Saint Joseph's Abbey outside Worcester, Massachusetts. I marked the Ezekiel manuscript as a legal defense document so I could keep it with me in jail on two occasions when I served brief sentences for protesting the Trident and Seawolf submarines. Some other images came from the "Mayonnaise Series." (These were drawings I made on scraps of paper in the New York City lockup after a protest on Martin Luther King Day against military spending done on the back of the poor. As I was lying, handcuffed, on the floor of a cell built for thirty but holding seventy, I drew — with a match and my fingers, using dirty mayonnaise mixed with floor grease for "paint" — the faces of those around me.) As I worked on the Ezekiel Series, I also began to feverishly collect relevant magazine and newspaper photos. I plowed through my photo archive and took many new photographs as I needed them to tell the story. I was inspired by and decided to incorporate some of Jim Harvey's photos of the people of El Salvador. I simply reached out for relevant contemporary images, and as I did one kept leading to the next and to an outburst of associations. I wanted this series to be in the realm of the commonplace and the teachable/immediately available — both visually and spiritually. This is the sense I gained from Dan's manuscript on Ezekiel. Simply, this is a book about us in our present time and place.

I began placing the five-inch by seven-inch Ezekiel proofs in groups of four, six, and even eight plates printed together. Some proofs were in black and white, others in earth colors, while others were complex multicolor plates. It soon became clear to me that this body of work was emerging like a film, where images return and reemerge and are juxtaposed with one another in different or new ways like a visual primal rhythm.

Throughout my work on the series, I was encouraged by many students of mine and friends. My strongest support and keenest criticism continue to come from my wife, Andrea. Our five-year-old daughter, Nora Marie, is always an inspiration when she is working side by side with me on her own etching plate. When my technique becomes too involved, my daughter teaches me simplicity.

After creating nearly three hundred proofs in the series, I decided on the group printed in this book. The etchings break down into four different but interchangeable categories: vision, suffering, politics, and healing. I invite readers to put their own words to the images. My Ezekiel Series etchings are really much more than illustrations of Dan Berrigan's manuscript. The artworks are images that invite us to go deeper into the meaning of these pages and scripture.

TOM LEWIS-BORBELY

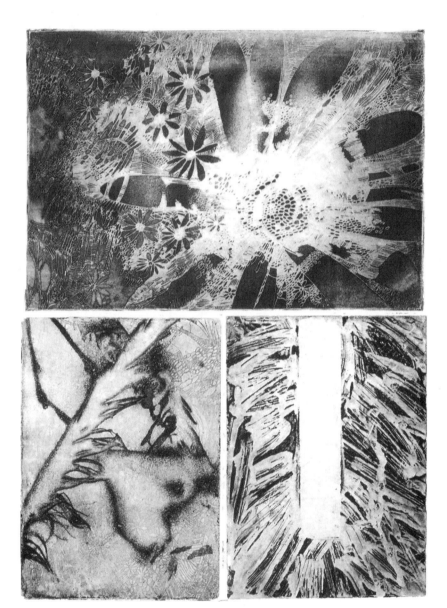

Preface

Ezekiel: Vision in the Dust

A burning question arose in the course of this study: Why does the Book of Ezekiel seem such a hard field to plough, why so emotionally draining? Why the nagging sense that we are being dragged along in harness, without the lightness of spirit we have come to expect from pondering the lives and works of the prophets?

It came to this. Perhaps the sense has something to do with the un-relieved doom and gloom imagery, the tirades (Ezekiel's own or God's, it seems not to matter which), Yahweh unyielding as a gelid Mount Olympus, thunderbolts let loose in all directions. So little of mercy or compassion or relief!

◆ ◆ ◆

The temple itself hardly escapes from a fierce critique. Ezekiel speaks again and again of the idolatries that were celebrated in the precincts — abominations that he, Isaiah, and Jeremiah are at one in insisting brought the temple down and down, a rubble.

Ironies aplenty!

◆ ◆ ◆

We long, in sum, for some relief, for something of hope perhaps. For a continuity of vision and emotion, instead of nightmarish episodes that seem designed only to fray the spirit. For the suavity and tenderness of an Isaiah or a Hosea.

For a sense that, all said and done, despite our follies and furies, God loves what God has brought into being. A sense that the human adventure is not a total loss!

◆ ◆ ◆

There is also Ezekiel's report on Yahweh to be coped with.

The suspicion arises that the divine temperament here presented exists solely, or to be charitable, primarily, in the eye of the beholder!

Yet we long to hear that love may after all prevail. That our sorry tribe is not beyond redeeming. That the shambles we have made of fair creation may be healed, that our bloodletting be stanched, that we be set free from the pit of nuclear madness.

◆ ◆ ◆

Ezekiel seems to me the most puzzling of the visionary Great Four, a seer whose logic and behavior lie all but beyond grasping.

Can this be a clue — that Ezekiel is the one most abused by Yahweh?

◆ ◆ ◆

Ezekiel, gloomy partisan of doom!

He is a priest. He loves the temple, even as he abominates the religion that drones on under the exalted roof.

Inevitably, in view of his diatribes, he is taken for a renegade by the priestly caste — who, noblesse oblige, much prefer that the fraternity maintain a common front.

◆ ◆ ◆

His peers are dismayed, chagrined. How, they ask in disbelief, can the great temple, its priestly bloodline, have produced so sour a spirit?

He seems to have fallen bodily from another planet.

◆ ◆ ◆

We seek clues.

Ezekiel, we have suggested, is mightily put upon. He is the first prophet to undergo a bitter exile, to speak from outside Israel. In the midst of his suffering people, he raises three questions:

1. What does it mean to confront the idols?

2. What is the spiritual impact of the idols on ourselves, whose only prospect is exile, or worse — who are actually driven forth? and

3. Have we, whether in exile or at home, submitted to an amoral assimilation, covertly or openly welcoming the idols, whether foreign or domestic?

Faced with such weighty questions, facing them for the most part alone, surrounded by a people gone slack and guileful, what is such a one as Ezekiel to do?

Here and there in Jerusalem, in the market, on the public street, at the city gate, he stages a series of bizarre pantomimes. Some are revolting; most are incomprehensible. No matter. He undertakes each with the tremendous concentration of a child or a madman.

◆ ◆ ◆

The reaction is predictable: indifference, laughter, scorn, rancorous hostility.

But of all this he was forewarned. Nothing would come of his best effort. Neither applause nor attentiveness nor conversion of heart would be the fruit of his street theater.

He can hope to bring a change of heart to very few, at best; most will turn away in contempt. And the worst comes to pass. He wears a stigma, marked as a fool or a madman.

◆ ◆ ◆

And in our day, psychoanalysis keeps the ancient verdict of the rabbis and scholars humming along.

With, of course, a twist of the blade. Ezekiel, it would seem, is a stunning candidate for this or that brain autopsy.

According to those reputed to know, he is afflicted with any (or all!) of the following diseases of the mind: he is "psychotic, paranoid, narcissistic, masochistic...." He has "fantasies of castration, unconscious sexual regression, delusions of persecution or of grandeur" — or any convergence of the above.

◆ ◆ ◆

No wonder the lowness of spirit! A discredited priest amid a culture whose elders and priests are icons of power and rectitude.

The temple, with its worship and commerce (or perhaps better, its worshipful commerce), presupposes, melds with, presumably even creates public prosperity.

The priestly version of the good life, of the public weal, holds firm.

Such a one as Ezekiel, courting disgrace and controversy, counts for little or nothing.

◆ ◆ ◆

It is the priests who construct the prevailing myths and images, dramas, mimes, call them what one will. These include the sonorous liturgies, the ebb and flow of commerce, a religious blessing accorded foreign alliances, approval of military shows of force. The star of David on the coinage, the star of David riding above the armies!

From these arise notions, commonly held, unassailable, of civic virtue and social pride (notions that centuries later would hold firm, be invoked in religious terms also, as a kind of "predestination of the prosperous").

◆ ◆ ◆

Self-understanding or self-delusion?

The citizens are urged to celebrate their entitlement, to revere the nation as preeminent, to hold their heads high. Are they not a great power in the world? Is not every public gesture a mark of civility, more, of benignity? Are not their wars, admittedly numerous, reluctantly undertaken, and this with a single purpose: to reduce or remove the wickedness of others? Are not their leaders the chosen among the chosen, their citizenry singularly fortunate and free?

◆ ◆ ◆

Enter now the little street dramas of Ezekiel, clumsy and stark, unfolding a countervailing myth of some moment.

The myth is outrageous.

Social rot, he insists, is underway. Injustice and greed and lust and violence and spiritual numbing infect the populace.

The poor are ignored and despised; justice is a lost cause; might makes right.

For this cause, disaster lurks.

A great military machine batters at the gates of Jerusalem.

◆ ◆ ◆

His warnings are dire, he flails out in all directions. The elite and power brokers, the militarists and the rich, the priests who confer a blessing on crime and default — these are doomed. They will be scattered like chaff to the four winds.

Thus, in sum, the drama, the faith, the method of Ezekiel.

One is put in mind of his Greek contemporaries, the tragedians Sophocles and Aeschylus. The house of Atreus is not unlike Jerusalem: the virtuous remnant, reduced perhaps to one (Antigone), and also doomed; the inflexible spoliator, judge, priest (Creon); and perhaps, most telling of all, the blind king (Oedipus), pursuing, even as he runs from, his own doom.

◆ ◆ ◆

But as to Ezekiel — Who lends ear to such matters, these pantomimes of a renegade priest?

A shouting match. "Call me what you will," Ezekiel cries. "I do the will of another; it is Yahweh who will have your moral befoulment cleansed!"

Willy-nilly, and much against his will, a survivor, discredited, miscast in the role of prophet, he cries into the contrary winds: "Murder most foul!"

◆ ◆ ◆

Appearance and assurances go counter: proclamations of national greatness, spectacular worship, the clink of money around the altar, church and state in sweet accord, repeated assurances; all manner of things are well. And he says nay. Disaster looms.

◆ ◆ ◆

Appearances to the contrary, official rhetoric to the contrary, worship to the contrary — all is not well.

Shout it, act it out, Ezekiel; shortly there will be very hell to pay.

The cause of the disaster must be proclaimed, diagnosed in detail.

Its cause lies in the heart, the heart of reality, social and personal.

Its effect? A wicked concordance of hearts and minds, of self-interest, greed, pride of place, bribery, profanation. In sum, the "system" at work.

Domination and death. These must be condemned.

◆ ◆ ◆

A war of myths is inevitable.

And Ezekiel stands for the most part alone. No faithful Baruch, friend of Jeremiah, at hand.

He has for resource body language, images, dramatic symbols, his wild and woolly street theater.

And all infused with such passion for the truth, as to set an arctic sea afire.

But not the human heart.

◆ ◆ ◆

Over against him stands a wall, daunting, seemingly impregnable; its squared blocks are the temple priesthood, money aplenty, imperial pretensions, the nobles, the armed forces — an awesome amalgam of power.

Beat against it he may, all in vain.

◆ ◆ ◆

Ezekiel beats and beats. He stages a mime of the common plight — spiritual illness, imminent disaster.

His dramas strike fiercely.

All the more fiercely, one ventures, because of his austere detachment.

He cares not a whit for an outcome favorable to himself, for influence or affluence or a slice of worldly power. A most detached man — and for that, the more dangerous!

◆ ◆ ◆

There is a strong implication that in playing the wise fool, Ezekiel is taking the social illness to himself.

Taking death to himself. The cruelest cut of all is predicted by Yahweh: the death of Ezekiel's wife.

She is taken from him, and he is forbidden all rituals of mourning.

With the prohibition we enter an area that lies far beyond street theater.

A grievous personal loss is inflicted, then extended into a parable of events to come.

◆ ◆ ◆

Even as they wonder at the prophet's demeanor, the people must learn the meaning of his stoicism.

The meaning: in days to come, there will be a redundancy of death in the land. All access to grief will be cut off. Numbing and indifference will freeze the heart. Self-preservation will obsess the survivors.

◆ ◆ ◆

And yet disaster is not all.

So complex, so nuanced, so unpredictable is this Ezekiel. We had almost neglected to credit a hunch. Surely there are other aspects of reality than death and catastrophe (one almost thought, other aspects of Yahweh)!

Those second thoughts intrude, nagging and wonderful.

◆ ◆ ◆

We shall hear of other, far different themes from Ezekiel. Despite the long night, a dawn. Doom is not all, not even nearly all! Light breaks, words of relief, hope, recourse, restoration.

Long delayed, and for that all the more striking.

As though these were indeed the point of it all, the meaning long hidden, the clue to the mysterious ways of Yahweh.

As though the long dolor were no more than a prelude, an inaugural discipline. After all, hope.

◆ ◆ ◆

Thus we are granted an inkling of the final righting of things.

Despite all, love prevails. The city is restored. The temple is to be built anew.

Restoration is both a fact and a symbol. We humans are to be rendered worthy — "rendered" literally in the furious furnace of adversity. Change of heart on our part has wrought a change of the heart of Yahweh. That God, wreaker of havoc, implacable witness of our wrongdoing, Olympian, disdaining, indignant — look, is at our side, is transformed; friend, counselor, lover.

◆ ◆ ◆

For generations, we are told, the rabbis held fast to weighty objections against the prophecies of Ezekiel.

They fought strenuously against the inclusion of his oracles in the canon of scripture.

Their objection seems on the face of it bizarre. It came to this: what he saw (or claimed to see — it came to the same thing), he recounted.

Easter Saturday, April 10, 1997

Introduction

With Ezekiel the great era of the prophets is in full tide. And what a relief, after the predatory era of Judges and Kings!

The heavens opened before him, a vision appeared, sublime and grandiloquent. The vision, ironically granted in exile, is the first in a series of opaque, even hallucinatory, images.

Ezekiel embraces his vocation, pays dearly for it, passes it on.

◆ ◆ ◆

His own tradition long has distrusted him, sought to exclude him from the canon.

Even today his code all but resists breaking; one reverts time and again to the offensive, shocking vision that strikes like lightning in the opening verses.

◆ ◆ ◆

The mimes he must perform — humiliating, absurd. It is as though Yahweh would pull him down, a sort of public clown, wan and dispirited, possibly mildly insane.

What he must undergo to lay open the wounds of soul and society!

He is bidden to "lie on your left side, . . . lie on your right side," to "clap your hands, stamp your feet, and cry 'alas!' . . ."

In fine, he must show in his humiliated body, for the sake of the body politic, what is to come — exile. Yahweh instructs: "Dig a hole in the wall and pass through it. While they look on, shoulder the burden and set out in the darkness."

◆ ◆ ◆

Ezekiel was destined to hear a decree of Yahweh, iconoclastic words such as were uttered to no other prophet. They signaled what looked like God's ultimate repudiation of the people and the temple. (And he a priest, cherishing both temple and liturgy.)

The anger of Yahweh came to an unexampled, dreadful climax (we shall see in some detail why). Like a gravely offended regent, Yahweh abandoned the holy place.

It seemed like the end of the world; and to all appearances it was. An era was crashing about the prophet's head.

The land was overrun by a merciless enemy, bent on extermination. And the people, whose proud boast was of a special status before God, were rendered — literally — godless. By God himself.

◆ ◆ ◆

At the point of disaster, Ezekiel is commanded to accompany his repudiated people into exile.

And it is in Babylon that he receives his vision and its charge. A cruel setting for his vocation; he alone among the prophets is anointed outside Jerusalem.

He must taste the fate of his people, to the lees. It is as though nothing of relief or repentance could befall until the worst had come to pass.

Or from another point of view, it is from "the remnant," those who have lost all, the despised and enslaved, that a human future will take form.

◆ ◆ ◆

As to those images of his: after initial shock, they seem apt and helpful. What a relief, one thinks — a new way of seeing, of understanding!

As when, immediately after the initial vision, "a hand stretches out to me, in which was a written scroll.... Written on it was lamentation and wailing and woe."

He is instructed to "eat the scroll," which he finds (and so strangely, given its purport) "sweet as honey in the mouth."

Could it be that the image is a deliberate oxymoron? To this effect: the truth (exile is inevitable) is a bitter dose indeed. Still, truth is a gift, especially so in face of prevarication and cover-up. So there is sweetness too.

The truth: quite a menu. The strong image of scripture as literal food, filling mouth and gut with its suave vitality!

◆ ◆ ◆

His image of a whitewashed wall — a wall that like Israel itself barely stands erect, is cracked and unsteady. And must be repaired, if not totally rebuilt.

The image is drawn out, dramatic, wonderfully apt and biting.

A coven of false prophets arrives at the wall. They are sedulous, skilled — in covering the truth over. They carry big brushes and pails. A touch here, a stroke there — they set to work.

Soon the wall gleams like new!

But Ezekiel has news for them. The rains will roar down; the wall will collapse in a rubble.

Then what of the whitewashers and their silly talk of "all's well," of "peace, peace, when there is no peace"?

◆ ◆ ◆

A true prophet endures the divine thunderbolts. Ezekiel knew it, to the bone. He must suffer with his people. If he did not, how could he venture to speak for them?

Endurance, survival, bare and unsung, became his lot. Babylon, exile, the worst years. Nothing of shame or defeat was spared him.

Yet he was guiltless, faithful to the end.

◆ ◆ ◆

Still, failure was not the whole story.

There was also the great prevailing event at the start. Where others were rejected and cast aside, Ezekiel was singled out. From then on, he walked the sere landscape, stood firm, spoke an unrelenting word. He became a figure of redemption.

◆ ◆ ◆

The irony is overwhelming. God's historical choice of this people, once so firmly in place, seemingly irrecusable, was negated, canceled. Ezekiel alone was the chosen one.

That choice, election, vision, assurance: To what end was it granted?

"A figure of redemption." The meaning of the phrase is necessarily obscure, even as it is certain.

Perhaps this: his task was, against overwhelming odds, to keep hope alive.

Whether in Jerusalem or in Babylon, he uttered a word of hope. Of necessity it was a dark word, ominous, at times threatening. A terrible event hung over the horizon. The decision of Yahweh was irreversible; they must lose all.

In due time, yes, return, restoration would come to pass. But only in due time.

◆ ◆ ◆

And his people, who in their heyday had been deaf and blind to the word, at length achieved a wisdom of sorts, and responded.

Realization dawned, a new day after the bleakest of nights. Eventually it became clear that the repudiation by Yahweh was not final. A chastened people came to a new understanding. The exile was a disciplinary act, one phase of the long pilgrimage of sin and repentance.

◆ ◆ ◆

But at what price to the prophet! He was spared nothing.

In an unlikely, barren terrain of contempt and enslavement, he announced a further chapter of the saga. Relief was dawning; exile and despoilment were not to be granted the last word.

Such a mad hope!

It took the form of a supreme vision, of the "dry bones" scattered in the wasteland.

From exile, shame, defeat, a dead end — came the revelation.

We must understand that for Ezekiel's people, all evidence, rumor, the false promises of yea-sayers, everything that shored up a kind of cultural optimism had been swept away, dissolved. Despair rode the saddle of the world; life had become its own "worst case." Ah, then it was that the heart of Ezekiel saw and his tongue was loosened. Hope stood free, sang its song of prevailing.

◆ ◆ ◆

In a place of pure desolation, an entire ecology speaks of the prevailing of death. A sere landscape, dry bones. No sign of life.

And then — a sign. One after another, the bones stand upright, connect one to another, grow animate. Skulls speak aloud. And death, lodged in cadavers like a parasite, in institutions like a colony of termites — death shall have no dominion!

Ezekiel (or Yahweh) had cannily chosen the occasion and locale: in a place and time when death seemingly had won every round, death, in the end, loses.

Then and now, an image to confront (and confound!) a culture of death!

◆ ◆ ◆

What if, what if! What if, one thinks, we could take the image to heart, name it for our own, walk with the dead who walk again, keep on keeping on, confront those not so hidden persuaders, the principalities — the entire cultural apparatus of death!

◆ ◆ ◆

In my mind, gradually, as such thoughts occurred, the strange, even bizarre, quality of the Book of Ezekiel gradually dissolved. His riches emerged, Lazarine and large.

Yes. He became for me an absolutely crucial voice, to help me endure, to interpret, to lend a helping hand. To survive the times, times that seem unredeemable, mad, collapsing like a wall. Ezekiel: a figure of redemption, a companion and witness, someone to stand with us.

◆ ◆ ◆

I was grateful for this, perhaps a small favor: he allows room for a touch of madness, surrounded as we are by evidence of insanity in high places — addictions to death-dealing, domination, greed, ego, the forms of death that govern authority high and low today.

◆ ◆ ◆

Ezekiel, truth-teller, points to another way.

He resists every attempt to be "normalized, by wicked authority," "assimilated" by the world; he will not grow spiritually sodden; no business as usual, no war as usual, no waste and want as usual, no religious rote and rot as usual.

God, he declares, has another, far different, hope for creation, for ourselves.

For the "widow and orphan," the abused and condemned and forgotten, those who count for little or nothing, "lives of no value."

And we, the beneficiaries of such sanity, so talismanic an ancestor, can only give thanks.

Ezekiel

...

THE DIARY OF LOSS
Ezekiel 1

His story begins on an altogether sober note.

The priest Ezekiel set out to record a chronicle of the exile. The date is exactly noted.

(And shortly, lightning strikes from a clear sky. All explodes in vision.)

◆ ◆ ◆

He begins:

The fifth day, well I marked it, of the fourth month of the thirtieth year of our harsh exile.

I, the priest Ezekiel, was tenting with the other deportees by the Grand Canal, near Tel Aviv. We were in blank despair. (1:1)

◆ ◆ ◆

His first (recorded) vision gave the game away.

No word was spoken from on high; there was only an epiphany, sight of the ineffable One.

Ezekiel saw; he told what he *saw* — or as much as may be conveyed in words.

Whereas, like the other prophets, he was instructed to tell only — what he *heard*.

He disobeyed, or so it was adduced.

He was granted access to the Mystery. But then he fell from grace. He dared tell or write or allow to be written of "a Being, a Someone, a Glory, a brilliant human Silhouette," the One who was "seated on a throne" (1:26–28).

◆ ◆ ◆

This was accounted excessive, outrageous. He played with fire; he broke a taboo.

And the question: Would not the violation encourage others in a like direction, making him the father of a renegade tradition of "see and tell"?

3

◆ ◆ ◆

A choice looms. Is he to tell what he heard ("The word of the Lord
came to Ezekiel") — or what he saw ("I saw divine visions")?
In fact he conveys nothing of this "word."
Precise Ezekiel quickly loses it.

◆ ◆ ◆

VISION

The hand of Yahweh rested upon me.
Heavy, heavy, a hundredweight, a death.
This I saw, this — as if, as if...

Four winged creatures, their visages
human, leonine, bovine, aquiline.
Quick as lightning they came and went,
hither and yon as the spirit drove them.

And the bruit of their coming, their going!
It was a sea, raging in its chains,
a tumultuous army breaking camp —
the voice of God Almighty!

In wing and claw and hand and hoof
each holding fast
the wheel of a chariot!
The wheels — alive, flashing,
strangely sightful!

Crowning the chariot,
a vault of dazzling crystal.
And a throne.

Words fail and pale.

Seated there on high,
I saw
a Being,
a Someone,
a Glory,
a brilliant human Silhouette.

Like a stone sped from a hand
Like my own death.
I fell to the ground. (1:28)

The point of the vertiginous apparition? It is, despite all — reassurance.

It was granted, we are told, to hearten the exiles (more nearly, to hearten the "mere mortal" who beheld the Glory).

The vision is also a prelude. Ezekiel is shortly to receive his vocation.

◆ ◆ ◆

Another note: the vision is brilliantly corrective.

For their part (and no wonder), the exiles are lost in a landscape of sadness and reverie. The reality of God is fading into murky supposition, doubt, despair. Is God with us? Has God abandoned us?

This is a God who once on a time flourished, reigned supreme, conferred largesse.

But the goodness is all but lost in a mist of nostalgia, a time when the people and their God dwelt "at home," in the Jerusalem temple.

◆ ◆ ◆

Jealous, exclusive, tribal; a kind of domesticating of God had occurred.

We remark the effort of an entire culture, led by its priestly caste, to claim for itself alone the universal One, the God of Isaiah and the Psalmist.

In the heady days of prosperity, everything conspired to shore up the claim: worship, economics, polity, even military muscle. Yahweh belongs to ourselves and to no others! was the cry.

The echo died in a gale. Nothing remained of that.

◆ ◆ ◆

The city fell; the proud were enslaved and exiled. It was the time of Ezekiel. His fate, the fate of his people, one.

The past and its grandeurs were reduced to a nostalgic dream, blown about mercilessly by winds of mischance.

The temple was no more. So with economic and military might, long gone.

◆ ◆ ◆

In those days of glory, ill-gotten, misspent, and long gone, only a few among the people, remnant-spirits like Ezekiel, conducted their lives differently, resisted the polluted winds, embraced a way of personal and social powerlessness.

These were the skeptics, even deriders, of the conventional temple-religion. They yielded no dependence on the dominant system of economic and military might.

◆ ◆ ◆

Now the ground has slipped underfoot; helplessness is imposed on all, willy nilly.

The quondam votary-citizens are a people without a country: stripped, abused, shunted about like animals in the witless world.

◆ ◆ ◆

The good life went easy as the waters of Shiloah; it provoked little if any questioning of God.

Then a bitter pill: destruction, loss of an identity frivolously taken for granted, squandered.

And of a sudden, a very thicket of questions springs up: Where now is our God — the God of stability, a God who was both pivot and center, who made sense of our world? Where the God who appointed times and seasons, who set the stars in their place, who sent the sun up, and the moon? Where the God who guaranteed a covenantal commerce, free and easy, a Jacob's ladder, access to high heaven?

◆ ◆ ◆

Vanished, gone, no more. The sun is fallen to earth. Darkness reigns. The moon is in crazy disjunction. The earth has slipped out of orbit.

We are the lost.

◆ ◆ ◆

Now the questions, and the questioner Ezekiel.

The questions and questioner alike are loaded with humiliation and shame. Ezekiel the exile, among the exiles.

·And who are we now?

The memories, the pain. They shift like a continental plate. The world is an open wound, like the social psyche, and the personal.

◆ ◆ ◆

A prelude to wisdom?

In any case, a further question haunts us: Who were we then?

◆ ◆ ◆

The question of Job is now our own.

Only exile, a vast reversal of fortune, could have made it our own. Behold us and weep. We, the chosen and favored, uprooted in a dolorous going forth, and no return in prospect.

Is this plight of ours no more than a chancy roll of the dice?

Or is there a God who hearkens?

◆ ◆ ◆

Well then, all this being so, says God (thereby allowing a measure of light upon a dark matter), let us take counsel.

Are My people to yield before this low mood, this onslaught of despair?

Have the gods of Babylon prevailed, who long before the catastrophe ranged free and far, invaded Jerusalem, laid claim, found ready worshipers there?

Have the exiles quite lost heart, lost a sense of me?

Has it come to this: that for them, I have ceased to exist?

And is this possible: that my rumination reach their ears, and in the breach serve for an answer of sorts, a comfort, though a cold one?

◆ ◆ ◆

Well, I, Yahweh, know of a certain mortal, valiant, febrile amid this disheartened tribe. A priest of possibilities, of stubborn will.

My eye rests on him. How his mood gleams and darkens, how he loses heart — and yet takes heart.

Volatile he is, shifting this way and that as though above a chasm, between hope and funerary darkness.

A man, in sum, of no small quality.

Something of hope survives in him; he does not yield to misapprehended doom, digging beforehand his own grave.

Nor is his mind a kind of mass grave in which despair would lodge the corpses of a people.

He has not caved in under adversity, not grown hollow.

No tabula rasa! Passionate, bellowing, eccentric. Ezekiel. I know him.

◆ ◆ ◆

He will not play hide and seek with me, will not ape Jonah, glib, gloomy browed, sour with resentment — because forsooth, I refuse to yield before his petulance!

No, the eyes of Ezekiel are open.

I will fill them.

With angelic spirits, the chariot and throne, the bones, dry bones.

THE DEAF HEAR NOT
Ezekiel 2

"Human one, stand up. I would speak with you."
The holy One breathed on me, and I stood.
"I am sending you to a rebellious people.
They have stopped their ears;
their hearts are adamant;
they are blind as the ancestral dead.
To these I send you.

> And a warning: as to my word,
> they will hear nothing,
> will mick-mock and turn away,
> morose, muttering, contemptuous;
> look to yourself, Ezekiel,
> you've lowered your ars
> in a nest of scorpions!
>
> "Ignore them,
> their moral lunacy.
> Utter my word.
> At least they will know
> a prophet stands in their midst!"
>
> A hand came toward me.
> It held a scroll.
> I read the words.
> It was as though a quill
> were dipped in tears or blood;
> as though grief, wailing,
> rose from the page. (2:1–10)

◆ ◆ ◆

For such as Ezekiel there is no way out.

No excuse will do, no caviling. The word must be spoken, the truth of things, truth of the world, of worldly wiles — and this, even as the wily seem utterly to prevail.

Even as they invade the sanctuary, bring shame upon the holy place, render the worshipers shameful.

◆ ◆ ◆

This is the sorrowful sequence of events.

No sooner is the word of God spoken than it is discarded, disobeyed, explained away, ideologized, ridiculed.

Then and now, belike?

The word dies on the air.

◆ ◆ ◆

And yet, and yet, Ezekiel must speak, though his life has become a great non sequitur.

He is to speak "as though," a fiction surpassing the awful fact, overvaulting it, ignoring it, despising it.

To speak with confidence and force and sangfroid and valiance.

To speak as though a favorable outcome were assured. As though in virtue of the word of God his hearers would grow thoughtful,

attentive, obedient. As though his auditors would imitate those unlikely Ninevehans who hearkened, one and all, "humans and beasts,"
to Jonah.

As though he too were sent to a Nineveh, and at his word the great
city were shortly convulsed as though by a quake, and converted.

◆ ◆ ◆

Nothing of this, not a whit.

And yet the command is not revoked, not for a moment.

The word must be spoken. In spite of all.

This is the passion of Yahweh, in more senses than one: that the truth
be made available.

Not that the word be hearkened to. That it be spoken.

◆ ◆ ◆

That word is a mercy, and it is merciless.

A judgment, a sign of contradiction, a wound and its healing.

And this is the passion of Ezekiel (in more senses than one) and of
his kind: that in a fallen world, in which truth and justice are perennial
strangers, the truth be spoken.

Even though in such a world, the truth will be granted no hearing.

◆ ◆ ◆

What then of this mere human, Ezekiel? How is he to shoulder so
heavy a burden, bewildered, uprooted as he is, in no wise spared the
fate of the exiles?

◆ ◆ ◆

He is not "like the others."

Let this be insisted on: the hand that lies heavy on him creates a difference in him. A difference that draws him forth like a blade Excalibur,
first in Jerusalem, then in exile.

A difference that is both burden and credential, that fits him for a
public role — and brings with it enormous pain.

◆ ◆ ◆

Unlike the others.

His affective life, passions, heart, mind, are blessed, focused, put to
a vocation of note.

He is transformed by the word entrusted to him. He is enabled to
live by the word; he becomes skilled and courageous, in view of and
speaking that word, in season and out.

◆ ◆ ◆

Who of us (we question ourselves in confusion of spirit), who of us could persevere in such a vocation, its outcome plainly unwrapped beforehand?

The outcome; it will all come to nothing. Your life will come to nothing. It is hereby traced on the air before all eyes, a virtual zero.

◆ ◆ ◆

And I reflect: "as to outcome," the lives of many of us have come to — very nearly nothing. Our best efforts have altered nothing in the horrid draconian drama of war and war preparation.

I think of the arrests over the years, the judicial processes, interminable, splenetic, tedious, utterly capricious, the long sentences meted out to family and friends.

And despite all that, the Wrecking Machine rolls on, an engine of ruin. No effort of ourselves (no effort of God?) serves to impede or halt it.

◆ ◆ ◆

Thus, as to main theme, goes our story. In certain crucial aspects it is similar to the story of Ezekiel, required as we are also to accept a desolate outcome — in his case stated beforehand, in ours woefully visible in the breach.

Ezekiel survives the outcome. So will we.

◆ ◆ ◆

The outcome: the word whose agent we are, whose credential we bear, changes precisely nothing of the downward spiral of violence.

A dilemma therefore, then and now.

For his part, Ezekiel cannot in principle walk the way of the world. And the world of the priests and people, in Jerusalem or in exile, refuses to walk the way of the word.

A stalemate is inevitable, more, a tragedy.

Is it to be wondered that the word will stick in his throat, that he will grow now mute, now wild and frenzied, miming like a madman the public madness?

Now and then, be it confessed, we too grow wild and frenzied.

◆ ◆ ◆

We consider his plight, his bitter portion.

From a nebbish, a fainéant, he becomes a chosen one; from a nameless deportee, a guardian of the word.

He longs passionately to fulfill God's hope. Yet he is told of the contempt to be accorded that hope. A contempt that will fall heavily on himself.

Sent, deputized, appointed, anointed to speak up.

And his words, like birds in the gun-sights of hunters, will fall from the air.

MORTAL ONE, EAT THE SCROLL
Ezekiel 3

And yet, the word did not die. Here it lies in our hands, heartening, vivid, lucid.

Someone heard, set down the word, published it abroad.

In time his oracles were canonized. They have reached us.

Always that ray of light, an exception to the awful rule, the curse.

◆ ◆ ◆

"Mortal one," said Yahweh, "eat the scroll. Then go, speak to the people."

Said: "My angel touched the lips of Isaiah with a burning coal; I have touched the lips of Jeremiah. These have spoken my word; so must you. Eat the scroll."

I ate; the words were sweet as honey in my mouth. (3:1–3)

◆ ◆ ◆

The bitterness of Yahweh contrives an argument a fortiori.

In this wise: if I were sending you among a foreign people, and you knew not a word of their language — even such as they would respect you, would strive to decipher your message.

But these, my own, the apple of my eye — they turn a deaf ear; they shrug and walk away. Hard of heart!

◆ ◆ ◆

"You shall be harder than they, hard as adamant.

Engrave my words on your heart, a mantra and meditation.

Every utterance of yours must begin this way: 'Yahweh says thus and so.'

Say it. I would hear you say it.

'Yahweh says thus and so.' Let them hear you say it. Whether they obey or disobey. God has spoken."

A mighty thunder clove the heavens, and a voice from the thunder: "All glory to Yahweh!"

The thunder was the clashing of wings, the mighty creatures who upbore the chariot.

And the spirit bore me off.

What lay ahead, what terrors!
I was back among the exiles, near the Grand Canal.
Bitterness and anger possessed me.
Seven days I abode there speechless, depleted by what I had seen and heard. (3:8–15)

◆ ◆ ◆

Yahweh: Eat the scroll.
Me: Eat a scroll? I hear cries of grief, lamentations, groans. Whose cries, whose groans?
Yahweh: Anyone's, anywhere in the world. Bosnia, Somalia, Northern Ireland, Haiti.
Myself: Your own?
Yahweh: My own tears.
Me: Because no one hears?
Yahweh: Because no one hears.
Me: Can I be of help?
Yahweh: Let this be said: Bosnia, Somalia, those who die, the innocents — they need not die; they should not. Abominable! My will undone!
Me: If only I could turn your weeping to — joy.
Yahweh: Eat the scroll.
Me: Sweet on the tongue, bitter in the guts! I read: "Love your enemies."
Yahweh: If only. If only...

◆ ◆ ◆
.

YOU, MY SENTINEL

Seven days went by.

Then once more, the word of Yahweh.
Said: "Ezekiel, come to Jerusalem.
An army, its sentinels night and day on the qui vive, hems the city.
I appoint you in a like image: a watchman, alert for the well-being of your people.
My warning take to heart, and convey.
Thus: evil, in yourselves or others, is punishable by death." (3:17ff.)

◆ ◆ ◆

Read the ethic thus: evil is the failure of a virtuous man to warn the wicked.

If the wickedness continue, death is the outcome for the evildoer —
as well as for that one who failed to speak.

But suppose a warning is issued the evildoer, and he mends nothing
of his conduct. And so dies.

In such case, only he is responsible for his death.

◆ ◆ ◆

Suppose, on the other hand, a virtuous man turns to evil. Now his
previous good works count for nothing; he will die.

And if no warning was issued, I hold the one who failed to speak
responsible.

If, on the contrary, such a one hearkens to the warning, he will live.
And so will the one who chastised him.

Word of Yahweh.

◆ ◆ ◆

Passing strange.

In the space of a few pages of Ezekiel's diary, recording a mere seven
days, we have passed from ecstasy to ethics.

The chariot has indeed swung low, and hardly sweetly.

Chariot? It is now a pulpit of sorts; or perhaps a podium.

A tough magister stands there. And an unequivocal lesson is driven
home (in more detail in chapter 33), uttered by the Prime Moral
Theologian of all!

◆ ◆ ◆

No more visions, at least not for awhile.

As the Buddha says: after the ecstasy, the laundry.

Now Ezekiel (and we as well) face — accountability, the quotidian,
the moral import of behavior, individual and social.

The lesson is harsh and disconcertingly clear.

It is delivered to a people on whose behalf, one would think,
considerable leeway should be allowed.

And why not? Shall victims and slaves lie under a law that were more
justly promulgated, one thinks, against invaders and persecutors?

◆ ◆ ◆

We ponder the situation.

The former elite of Jerusalem are beleaguered, psychologically and
spiritually uprooted, transported afar.

And yet the law, the law! It affects the exiles disconcertingly, directly;
it judges them.

Their harsh duress by no means exempts them from accountability.
Quite the opposite.

The language is rigorous. God insists on righteous conduct — even in circumstances that hold the people close as a mailed fist.

◆ ◆ ◆

What then is the point, the drift of the law?

It might well lie in another direction than legalistic rigor.

Thus Yahweh might vindicate the dignity of the expelled, deprived as they are of symbols and possessions and emoluments, of homeland and temple, all bespeaking an honored place in the world and before Yahweh.

The implication is in their favor. If slaves and free alike stand under judgment, then the slaves, including the slave Ezekiel, stand free.

◆ ◆ ◆

There is yet another angle to the moral teaching.

One thinks of its attentiveness to accountability, to sin and consequence. Through the entire book, the connection holds firm, warp and woof. The weaving of a coherent story, a history.

Thus we are reminded again and again that the destruction of the city and the consequent exile are by no means or primarily due to the violence of invading empires.

Like a shadow of the Eumenides dogging an evildoer, disasters follow on the wickedness and crime of the chosen.

◆ ◆ ◆

For every curse, supplanting it, canceling it — a blessing.

The fall of the holy city, the banishment, was curse indeed.

And yet, and yet. If the word of God is to gain a hearing, it must wait on a better mind. Must wait on, even create, a circumstance far different than the self-aggrandizing prosperity of so-called normal times.

Must wait on an understanding purified by travail and suffering.

◆ ◆ ◆

As for Ezekiel, we note that he walks two worlds of experience. First comes the vision of the chariot, the seraphs, Yahweh.

Then a pronunciamento, an austere word concerning who stands where before God — meriting judgment or blessing.

◆ ◆ ◆

Insisting as Ezekiel does that the exiles are accountable, his self-understanding benefits; his conscience is expanded and clarified.

He is to be a kind of latter-day Moses, lawgiver and ecstatic, both.

Indeed he comes to know that the "law," rightly understood, is itself prophetic.

And the prophecies and visions and revelations are to issue in righteous behavior — that of Ezekiel first of all.

◆ ◆ ◆

Thus there comes to him the vision of the enthroned One; and later he hears intoned the law of just behavior. Two sides of a coin stamped, "Glory of God."

The coin is thrust in the palm of Ezekiel, bewildered and angrified though he be.

The coin is hot, newly minted. It burns his flesh.

Shall he accept it, trade in it?

◆ ◆ ◆

Not to be thought wonderful — he grinds his teeth; his guts are in revolt. Obey, submit he would not — and yet he must.

The superscription is traced in gold. Read it, believe it, walk with it: I, Yahweh, love you.

Or perhaps: I, Yahweh, am with you.

Against all contrary evidence thrust at your God (your broken word, your broken lives) — I am with you. Tell them so.

I grant visions in the dust.

And I hold you, visionary and people, accountable.

◆ ◆ ◆

Yahweh said: Here is a resume of the crimes, and the account due.

You thought to own me, a temple darling, a kept deity.

I could be assuaged, stroked, cozened by unctuous priests, meretricious acolytes.

So you concluded, so worshiped, ·so publicly behaved; an illusion thrice compounded.

"Our god" indeed.

Idols in the sanctuary, injustice abroad.

◆ ◆ ◆

It must all come down. I will bring it down, this house of cards upon whose prospering you have staked everything.

You have lost — everything.

I scatter you like a chaff to the four winds.

◆ ◆ ◆

SILENCE, SPEECH: ALL ONE

I, Ezekiel, was aghast. The Presence again, and the Voice.

He commands me to speak.

Then a contrary command: I must be silent.

This way and that I am shunted about.

First: Return, rejoin the exiles. Then: Retreat, close the door of the house.

Threats I heard, mutterings like sultry thunder "I shall utterly destroy this people, scatter them."

And then the brow of Yahweh cleared. The lightnings dispersed, skies cleared.

The promise: "Behold I am with them."

I, Ezekiel, am to make sense of both, of the oppositions, the contradictions.

Make sense, of no apparent sense.

Obey. Come what may.

It is the extremes that wound, that petrify the tongue, the will. Do this: forbear doing that.

Hasten abroad; stand stock still.

Speak with power. Then: Hush.

I am spinning in a gyre. This deity will drive me mad. (3:22ff.)

THEATER AT THE PUBLIC GATES
Ezekiel 4

Said: "Look to it, Ezekiel. My words go nowhere; they fall to ground like the hunters' winged prey.

Therefore. No more words.

You will mime the fall of the great city (which has already fallen, has become a Babylon).

A second death, so be it, after the first.

"Devise then the following. Miniature trenches, earthworks, camps, battering rams.

And you, heart and soul, play the part; stand fiercely over against them. Mime the besieger, the enemy.

It is my own part; play it to the hilt.

I stand against this people, I besiege them, I am their enemy.

"A drama of three acts.

First, mix a dough of tears and chaff; bake it over a fire of dried excrement.

Summon the people. Eat that sorry loaf, bread of exile, bread of slaves.

Bread also of consequence, leaven of the misbegotten and rebellious ones.

Then stand there, shake your fist like a madman against the city.

"Final act.

I bind you tight, hands and feet. Groan there, a captive for a space of forty days.

They will suffer, long and long, as many years." (4:1ff.)

 ## TEACH THIS GLIB PEOPLE
Ezekiel 5

On and on, the word:

"Mortal man, take in hand a sharp sword. Shave both head and beard. Divide the hair in three.

When the city falls under siege, burn a portion of the hair in public.

Walk about the city, scatter a handful to the winds. (I myself will follow you, sword drawn.)

Cast a portion of hair in the fire.

Tell the people: a day is nearing when in this city, parents will slay and eat their children, children the parents.

"This is the outcome, as night follows day.

The covenant is violated and held to scorn.

In consequence no one, nothing, is honored or cherished.

Baal in the sanctuary! injustice stalking the land!

"Speak to them, those Jerusalemites, once my people. Tell them the meaning of the mime.

Thus: a third will perish of plague and famine.

A third will fall under the sword.

And a third will be scattered to the winds and pursued with the sword. I have spoken.

"Now hear their talk, a mishmash of scorn and disbelief.

Ghastly, glib:

'Such could not happen to us!

'And this Ezekiel, his words are inflammatory, a firestorm of verbiage set aflame by a madman.

'The facts are plain, look around. We prosper, life is tranquil, normal.

'What could be thought more permanent, more firmly planted and prosperous than this "lifestyle" of ours?

'Religion, citizenship, walking to the common beat. A system, sensible and successful, which wins only plaudits, blessings.

'Upon the drumhead is tattooed — $$$$$. The drummer is followed by a mighty militia, weaponry thunders along on caissons.' "

Are objections voiced?

Of course; every generation spawns a few would-be Ezekiels.

Ruin, disaster! No nukes, war no more!

It is all familiar; one takes the long way round such malcontents.

The law too is circumspect, the police efficient. (5:1ff.)

◆ ◆ ◆

Let us imagine a group, contriving in a public place some rite of its own devising.

They mutter a Mass before this or that objectionable institution; or they anoint themselves with ash; or they plant trees or flowers or scatter grains about. Or again, they sprinkle the property with a red substance, which they insist is their own blood.

If matters stop there, we consider the perpetrators, though ill-advised (as even their religious compatriots agree), well within their rights.

◆ ◆ ◆

Ezekiel, we are told, hunkered down in a thoroughfare, and proceeded to shave in public. Then he wandered about the city, muttering to himself.

The spectacle bemused many; the bystanders were curious rather than hostile. Some lingered awhile, some drifted off in his wake.

It was all quite harmless; the authorities kept their distance.

This distempered spirit, for all his moan and groan, had broken no law.

If to his poor mind and truculent voice, reality was bleak and dark — surely he harmed no one but himself.

◆ ◆ ◆

The law is enlightened. Such antics hardly fall under judicial scrutiny. Rather, poor Ezekiel seems a fit subject for the alienists; let them deal with him.

Look now: he stands outside the city, shouting against the wind wild fulminations aimed at — the very mountains. Pitiful.

SHOUT TO THE HILLS!
Ezekiel 6

The eternal hills are summoned.

Word of Yahweh: "Your leaders and people take no account of me.

Turn then to the mountains. They are, after all, less stony, blank, than human hearts.

Among those gorges and valleys, the fauna will lift their heads, startled by the cries reverberating along the corridors of silence. Perhaps the very flora will bend obeisant, as though under the blast of a trump." (6:1ff.)

◆ ◆ ◆

There is, to be sure, more to the scene and its summons than a rural fantasy.

The mountains are polluted with shrines. Creation itself has been transformed, degraded.

◆ ◆ ◆

These are like mountains of the moon, loony, menacing, seductive, pocked with false symbols, with fantastic altars, symbols of untruths that turn minds awry. Nature is included in the desecration; the mountains literally are transformed, are rendered complicit with the Fall.

They shield idolaters and their idols.

So they too must be included in judgment, in an ecology of accountability, along with their human collaborators.

◆ ◆ ◆

This also is to be understood. The abominations of the "high places" are in no sense deviations from the temple-religion.

The mountain shrines are simply the outposts of temple and synagogue.

Ironically, they enact abroad the rites that proceed in the temple of Jerusalem.

(One thinks in this regard of chapels erected on foreign bases; the rites and celebrations and invocations of whatever god might be thought to bless the mephitic enterprises of empire.)

◆ ◆ ◆

Yahweh has drawn the awful connection: "You have soiled my sanctuary with horrors and abominable practices"; and later: "I will destroy the places where people worship idols."

LOOK TO IT, ISRAEL
Ezekiel 7

"Like wild dogs
off the leash —
across the land
furies I will loose!

"Barbarians —
pillage the great homes,
profane the sanctuary —
I close my eyes!
No avail!

"Hands fall helpless,
knees shaking —
witless,
you flee and flee,
like flocks of affrighted doves!

"Terror reigns —
sackcloth for shroud,
ash to ash, dust to dust.

"Silver a curse,
gold a dross —
despair, confusion of spirit.

"You cry: Peace!
Peace flees the land;
priesthood sterile,
elders defaulting.

"Even as you have judged,
be judged!
Yes, at long last,
Yahweh you will know!" (7:5–12)

♦ ♦ ♦

We have heard it before, frequent, unyielding, one would think it the very substance of prophecy — threat and scalding anger, disaster impending.

At the least it can be said: this God is no neutral, no bystander in the precincts of human conduct.

◆ ◆ ◆

A sunny morning in May. Springtime raises its promise, a full cup to the lip. I look out upon my street; every condition of life, every age and race! People, decent and peaceable, going about their modest Sunday diversions.

One thinks; if this street, Broadway, these few blocks comprising my neighborhood, these few thousand people, were taken as image and microcosm of the world — why then there could be no horror named Bosnia, no slaughter in the Gulf, no famine in Somalia, no bloodletting in Rwanda, no drownings of desperate refugees off the coast of Haiti.

Nor could there be warrant for the terrifying words spoken by Yahweh, in contention against his own.

But, but. A warrant is served:

> Vietnam, Somalia, Bosnia, Iraq —
> these are no confabulations
> of a madman Ezekiel,
> sputtering like a lit
> arrow tip
> aimed with gimlet eye
> at the innocents of earth.

No, the world is more complex by far.

From this height, my street and its pilgrims resemble a clutch of mechanical dolls, walking abroad in the innocent morning, for chores, for pleasure, for a meed of bracing air.

Only connect!

Ezekiel is a great one, a confounding one, for connections.

◆ ◆ ◆

Which is to say:

declarations of innocence,
presumptions of such,
children cherished,
a certain modest (or immodest) prospering of some,
churchgoing (or not),
the slowing of quotidian rhythms to a pace befitting Sunday,

a certain version of the world fatly reinforced by five pounds of
   New York Times,
borne homeward like a suckling pig from market —
these hardly can be adduced as establishing immunity
from the scalding indictment.
Quite otherwise alas.

◆ ◆ ◆

The *Times,* flat out with its cultural and political and economic (and yes, religious) fiats, the leisure, the wild or tamed variety of humans (wild by weekday, tamed for the nonce), the clothing modest or flaunting, the churches like caves, shadowy, inviting aspiration and assurance: these are hailed forward, alas, as something other than evidence of justification, or a plain show of decency, of innocence.

They are in fact items of quite opposite character — evidence for the prosecution.

◆ ◆ ◆

I leave it to you (Ezekiel says Yahweh says), decent people all — I leave it to you.

Your "bible," all said, is a piggish secular version of the world, borne home, perused, made much or little of, then cast aside.

Sedulous voters, taxpayers, merchants, professors, politicos, generals, and weapons hucksters — they walk these streets too; they enter the church portals all (so it is understood) for sake of the common weal, the "family values."

◆ ◆ ◆

Generals
fresh from the works of
"collateral damage"
bow their heads,
receiving
as under a mild waterfall,
the benison,
neutral, mellifluous —
appalling.

How crack
the adamantine assurance?
How, Ezekiel,
roll the stone away, away?

Fire and fury!
white hot —

medals of "honor"
burn to the bone!

Snatch coins from pockets!
Yes,
children from mothers' arms!

Rend flesh from bones!
Lay siege to New York!
Famine, plague,
sword laid to throat!

The stone images,
martyrs, saints,
weep where they stand.

Behold,
    Yahweh on a swift cloud!
    Idols
    (money, swords, flags,
    utopias attainable
    Himalayan summits
    of pride of place)
    IDOLS
    one and all
    shudder where
    they stand,
    short-
    -ly
    top-
    -ple

ABOMINATIONS ABOUNDING
Ezekiel 8

Worship. The drone and mutter and music, the stench of animal blood, the lutes and violas and flutes, the covert yawns of priestly automatons, in sum, a self-serving necrophiliac charade....

"But I, Yahweh, will show you the heart of this matter. I will reveal hearts and minds."

Yahweh took me by hair of head, transported me on the instant to Jerusalem.

Behold an altar, an idol, monstrous; "the statue of jealousy, which stirs up jealousy." (8:1–3)

◆ ◆ ◆

An image, we are told, of the goddess Asherah, long before (and it was thought, once for all) removed by Josiah (2 Kings 23:6).

Not at all. It is set in place once more.

A statue of emulation, of ambiguity, teeming with implication.

Is Yahweh other than "a jealous God"? Shall this then be tolerated? Yahweh is furious. Shall he be supplanted?

The image is one of regression. The gods, put to death or to sleep, those pseudobeings whose power bespeaks our lust for death, stir where they lie.

They are the counterclaimants, the appetites, the genies who await the commands of nurslings, of spiritual infants.

They are the great supplanters. They lust after the worship of supplanters.

◆ ◆ ◆

Said Yahweh: "I will show you worse abominations."

Took me to the wall of the outer courtyard. Said: "Break through the wall." I did so.

Within, upon the walls, a smear and welter of unclean images, outrageous frescoes of beasts, serpents, birds, idols all.

And before the images stood the elders of Israel. Censers in hand, they paid obeisance to the beasts of the earth.

The smoke mounted on the air.

Yahweh spoke: "They say in their hearts: Yahweh sees nothing."

Said: "I will show you worse than this."

At the north gate stood a coven of women.

It was autumn; they were mourning the death of the corn god.

Finally, to the inner courtyard. There, between altar and porch, stood a score of men.

Backs to the altar of Yahweh, they faced the rising sun, and bowed in adoration.

Yahweh said: "Such things you behold. And the land is a volcano of violence." (8:6–17)

◆ ◆ ◆

It is an ancient theme, and a new one. And nowhere explored with more devastating clarity and detail than by visionary Ezekiel.

It is as though Yahweh were opening to the prophet, one by one, the secret chambers of the heart: of worshipers and elders alike. Break through the wall, force the door!

A devastating contrast is revealed.

In plain daylight, before the altar, one form of worship, the official one, was in progress.

And in the darkness below, in a kind of murky subconscious, behold the truth of things, giving the lie to the official worship above. Idolatry.

A truth which "official religion" guarded, concealed, itself enacted; the tribute paid the gods, their maleficences, the terrible "others."

Prophecy, the truth, the unbearable truth of things.

◆ ◆ ◆

Has there been in the Bible, or elsewhere, a more devastating unveiling of the human soul?

The idols loom there, principalities of the lower regions. They own the darkness; they own the heart of darkness, undisputed and contemptuous. They own the heart.

They are powerful, clairvoyant, drawing.

The terrible drama proceeds.

In due time the gods of darkness, like a species of deadly nightshade, will emerge from the underground, clairvoyant, claimant. They will succeed to the throne, to the holy place.

Then they will evict God.

◆ ◆ ◆

Ezekiel would have us know it. God will fare as his prophet fares — exiled, despised, a totem toppled. Before a greater power (for a time), before wickedness in the ascendant (for a time), God will yield and withdraw.

Then of all the recusant tribe, God counts on and summons one only, a heart faithful and parched like his own.

◆ ◆ ◆

God dethroned, disinherited, denied. And the solitary one who barely survives, to tell of such abominations.

These two a remnant indeed, Ezekiel and the God of the remnant, alike in misery and truth and fury.

◆ ◆ ◆

Is this what it means to be God in such a world?

Is this what it means to be godly in such a world?

Is this the guise that must be ours as well, the image offered here —
the rejected One and the solitary believer?

It is as though the two, exiled from time and this world, wandered
abroad in a lunar desert, seeking — What?

A welcome, a human face, relief — an Abraham perhaps, prospering
among his flocks; food and cool drink; an icon to inhabit?

SLAUGHTER, SWIFT AND SURE
Ezekiel 9

This city or that, it makes no difference, the decree falls.

The heart shrivels as the eye scans the awful page.

No indemnity is granted the quondam "holy city."

The mercy of God is beyond mercy; God has become an Alexander,
a Cyrus, a wrathful tyrant.

Spare no one: young or aged, men, women, children.

◆ ◆ ◆

The wicked said in their hearts: "Yahweh has left the city; he
sees nothing."

And Yahweh: "You have spoken well, you wicked ones.
Absent indeed, blind with tears!

You have cast me aside; see how I cast aside all compassion.
My eyes are bound up.

Blind as dame justice, justice is mine.

This I shall be to you: an exile, an absence, a hiatus of
existence, far from mercy and reconciling.

"Summon the executioners; let a scribe accompany them.

Take in account those who groan and weep at sight of the
abominations of this city. Mark a cross on their forehead.

And slay all the others.

Your bloody work starts here, in the sanctuary.

Pollute the place (it is already polluted) with the corpses of
those who have welcomed the idols." (9:4–10)

Yahweh's unresolved stony grief!

◆ ◆ ◆

Can one speak of true religion as evacuated of all anger?

"The world, the way it goes" — and ourselves grown callous, neutral
before high crime.

The innocents die, whether in war or aftermath of war.

The sanctions against medical aid, food, fuel, stand firm.

In such ways does an imperial culture ever so gradually (or quickly) define the communal morality, lay claim to conscience; its terms the only terms.

Few dissenting voices; and such as are raised, are ignored with ease.

◆ ◆ ◆

Ezekiel, that solitary dissenting voice. He lay prone, in tears, forehead pressed against the stones of creation.

> Pleading on behalf of the doomed,
> I sought the heart of Yahweh; it was turned to adamant.
> Mercy died in his throat.
> I, Ezekiel, became that part of Yahweh he would have no part of.
> I became his heart, and its heartbeat.
> And I availed nothing.
> There appeared the scribe, all in white, his slate in hand.
> Said: "The command is obeyed." (9:11)

ONCE MORE, THE LIVING CREATURES
Ezekiel 10

> Yahweh, to the cherubim:
> "Go take in hand coals of fire;
> scatter coals over the city."
>
> The winged creature
> took up the living coals
> and before my eyes, departed.
>
> I saw then the great chariot,
> wheels agleam like jewels.
> And the four creatures
> winged, agile, majestic.
>
> The face of the first, an angel;
> The second, human;
> the third, leonine;
> the fourth, a bird of prey. (10:2ff.)

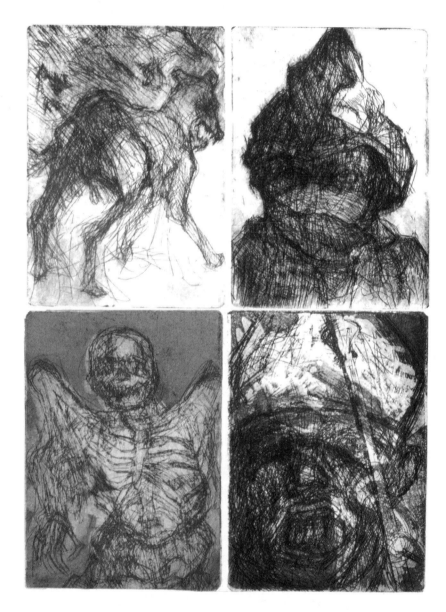

JUDGMENT FALLS ON THE GREAT ONES
Ezekiel 11

The spirit led me to the eastern gate.
There were gathered a knot of elders; among them a certain Pelatiah.
They stood conversing.
The city burned and burned.
Yahweh: "Behold the wicked elders of Jerusalem.
Their counsel is — mad;
Hear their babble: 'Well, we must set about building again!'

"Thus their confabulations: 'Jerusalem is a hot caldron indeed, and we alas, like meat in the pot.
Still, things could be worse; the pot protects the meat from the fire!'
Insolence!
This is the meat of your pot — the entire city aflame, the streets choked with corpses!
And you imagine yourselves safe and sound!
I will shortly drive you forth — into a phalanx of swords."

No sooner spoken, Pelatiah fell dead before me.
And I too fell to ground, crying out: "Yahweh, would you then destroy even the sorry remnant?"
No response.

Yahweh: "Mortal one, those who malinger in Jerusalem defame you and the exiles. They sneer; too bad for them, those others. They dwell far from Yahweh, too far.
And again, inflated like blowfish: to such as ourselves the future belongs.
Answer them. True, I have scattered many among the nations. For a time, for this awful time, I myself am their sanctuary.

"Remind the exiles of my promise.
I have scattered you; I will gather you. I will create in you a new heart and a new spirit.
I will excise your hearts of stone, mold in you a heart of flesh.
This shall be: you my people, I your God.

THEN
THE GLORY OF GOD
AROSE
ON THE WINGS OF CHERUBIM
AND DEPARTED FROM THE CITY.

And I, the spirit once more seized on me, transported me, back to my people in Babylon.

To them I recounted all I had been given to see. (11:1–25)

◆ ◆ ◆

There are those who languish afar, and those who die in the streets of Jerusalem.

And others, by hook or crook, survive and make do in the burning city.

Such eminences are skilled in survival; ways and means they come on, brands plucked from the fire.

Perhaps not all is lost! they exclaim.

Native to cunning and greed, they turn disaster around, to their own advantage.

◆ ◆ ◆

These wise worldlings of Jerusalem, active, advantaged amid the ashes.

A clutch of these, we are told, stand amid the firestorm and connive ways and means of salvaging their vast possessions.

Plain deaf, blind, numb they are to the suffering and death that ring them about.

◆ ◆ ◆

In a later scripture we are offered a reprise of this scene.

The elders of Ezekiel's time much resemble the merchants and captains of trade fleets told of in Revelation.

These moguls of world markets witness the fall of Babylon.

They stand there — "far off" we are told — "because they are afraid to share in her suffering" (18:11–19).

Guilty, bystanding, conjecturing, calculating, weighing their chances. The emotional distancing is obvious, disconcerting, true.

◆ ◆ ◆

The first preoccupation is a cool appraisal of the main issue — their endangered goods.

Damage must be reckoned up, loss against profit, red column and black.

◆ ◆ ◆

No question, be it marked, of the horrendous ruin accruing to others. Image, repute, chattels intact or restored — these are the only pressing questions.

Talk about generational sin: the elders in the ruined city, the great merchants and tycoons of Babylon!

For avarice and heartlessness, is there to be thought a notable difference between chosen and goy?

◆ ◆ ◆

A horrid memory recurs.

Toward the beginning of 1993, we Americans were subject to a military countdown. So many days, then so many hours. The clocks moved inexorably. There was no resolution.

Then war erupted in the Gulf.

And the perpetrators were quick to justify before the public their bloody undertaking.

In a flash the "just-war" theory was invoked, against all evidence. Was there evidence to the contrary? Throttle the media, enlist the churches, push the morality hard.

◆ ◆ ◆

Another instance. A religious cult in Waco, Texas, under siege and surveillance, dug itself in.

The members thus presented the "justice department" with an impasse.

Shortly a ghoulish decision was reached: the matter must be abruptly resolved.

With military finesse the camp was invaded, many children and adults died.

"Damage control" once more became the sole issue for the government — form, image, plausibility.

It is worth noting also that the decision to "go in" with full might was reached by a woman official, a Democrat serving Clinton.

Democrat, Republican, woman in charge or man, what difference?

The decision and its outcome resembled, with excruciating exactitude, a like situation and a like response by, say, a male official, a Republican, serving Bush or Reagan.

One and all, alike. Let the children, whether of Baghdad or Cuba or Waco, be deemed expendable, and perish.

◆ ◆ ◆

Thus do descendants of a certain type (whether sea captains, merchants, or officials of a later empire) ape the ethic of their ancestors: here identified as the "elders of Jerusalem."

Thus the atavism, the appalling consonance, no matter the period or culture, in the behavior of a certain brand of authority.

◆ ◆ ◆

Lives and deaths are weighed; many among the living are found wanting.

Perhaps their fault is a want of attachment to the law. Or perhaps they interfere with the normal functioning of the system. Or their conduct is found to bruise certain highly placed egos.

In any case, for one reason or another, their lives are declared expendable; there will be no compassion, no negotiating with these.

Their death is decreed. Alas, regretfully, their death is a "lesser evil."

◆ ◆ ◆

One notes the grisly emotional distancing, the inevitable (one is tempted to say genetic) reliance on violence as a social method.

They move, these merchants of death, governors of death, with the impatience of the weapons they create, aim, and discharge. Get the thing done with!

The guns in effect possess their possessors.

EXILE YAHWEH, EXILE EZEKIEL
Ezekiel 12

Said Yahweh:
"This people have eyes, and see nothing,
ears, and hear nothing.
Therefore a task for you
who see and hear aright:

"Take up a sack,
fill it with clothing and food.
Cover your face with a dark cloth.
At nightfall
heft the burden to shoulder.
Depart.
Wide-eyed, wondering,
they will seek explanation.
Offer none."

So I obeyed.

Toward evening I hefted a bundle,
broke through the wall of my house.

The people heard the commotion,
gathered, all eyes,
astonished, silent.

I set out, face covered,
blind as a bat at noon.

Whither and why?

God knows.
Like an Abraham
summoned,
I knew
nothing. . . .

Again instructed: "Ezekiel,
take bread in hand,
trembling.
   Lift a cup,
shuddering.
   Tell them:
   'You will eat in trembling,
drink, and quake —
   blindfolded, hands bound,
   scattered like a chaff
in merciless winds.' "

   Said:
   "Symbol of things to come.
   As you have mimed,
   so it will come to pass.
   Do they pay heed
   to you, to me?
   Hearken
   how they summon
   stale witticism —
   'Ho hum, day follows day,
   boredom and breath.
   Day alike day —
   all come to naught —
   prophecy? A nothing
   gone up in smoke.'

"Fond, foolish —
the end comes speedily!

Yahweh has spoken.
Never the less!
A remnant I will spare
to remember, to recount
woe, consequence." (12:1–26)

◆ ◆ ◆

"Prophecy, a nothing gone up in smoke."

Dare we translate the peoples' proverb as a kind of "interim ethic"?

By way of example. Let us concede for a moment that the words of Jesus concerning love of enemies are deserving of the honorable name Prophecy.

Granting the serious character of the love/enemy irony, and the clarity of the stated command — despite all this, a puzzling consequence occurs. Suppose that (the supposition is bound to be verified, alas) an offense or incursion contrary to "national interest" is adduced. An enemy is named — or is confabulated. War is in prospect.

And a number of ethical experts proceed to void the prophecy of Jesus of any moral weight. The theory of the "just war," that lively corpse, is dusted off and resuscitated.

"Ho hum, day follows day....Prophecy? A nothing gone up in smoke."

◆ ◆ ◆

An image suggests itself.

The words of the gospel are put to the fire. The heat generated fuels a kind of hot-air observation balloon. The vehicle rides high above earth.

The gospel, thus transmuted to hot air, keeps the airborne crew far above, distant from earth and time and terrain and the muck and reek of the human, its treachery, lunacy.

Yes, and far from its glory.

Who judges, who sees aright?

Alas, we soar the empyrean, above and beyond, cut loose from earth, from responsibility, from the interventions of faithful love.

◆ ◆ ◆

From a convenient distance, the riders find the chaos of the killing fields — regrettable of course; inevitable — also of course.

Aloft, a shrug of abstraction. We are, after all, "above all that," exempt.

Love of enemies? The dictum loses all commanding power.

PEACE, PEACE, WHEN THERE IS NO PEACE
Ezekiel 13

"Mortal one,
hear them cry, Yahweh, Yahweh!
Such perfidy!
        Preposterous
the conjuring, the persiflage!
        Peace! their cry —
hoarse in the throat —
        the throat of war.

"What think you?
        Circling the city,
quick, a wall goes up.
Stone on stone
in panic they raise it.
A fool's barricade,
loose, rattling
in war's rumor —
a paling of air,
the ghosts walk through!

"Or they seek
concealment, cover.
Workmen, broad brushes
dipped to the hilt, dripping
    whitewash.
    Nonetheless
    truth
    horridly seeps through —
        the stones drip blood.

"I, Yahweh,
storm that rickety wall,
hurricane, hailstone, torrent — I
rattle the flimsy wattle,
tumble it down,
bones, stones, a welter.
And the white washes away,
a corpse's cosmetic
beatitude.

"Lo
great ones of earth —
you I abrogate; I unmake
  you
  nonentities —
  your names
written in water." (13:1–16)

◆ ◆ ◆

Thus the first of the "unmaking" (unmasking) oracles — Ezekiel at his subversive, surreal best.

The image of the quaking unsteady wall is echoed by Isaiah.

And the "whitewash," the "cover-up," the concealment of shoddy work — we too have seen it.

All thanks to Yahweh the subverter, and the subversive servants of Yahweh! — thanks to those who kick the wall down or shoulder it aside, and so reveal "the filth, the dead men's bones."

THE DISSEMBLERS DEALT WITH
Ezekiel 14

Gray of mien and mind they came, the great ones seeking consultation with me, Ezekiel.

It was a gesture I could only judge ambiguous.

What had they to do with me, or for that matter, I with them?

Was I not the butt of their anger, playing. as I did the fool among the exiles, miming weirdly in public, our plight?

And again, are these elders to be accounted worthy of trust?

Some among them form cabals, pitifully scrambling after scraps of power, trading in misery, even collaborating with the tyrant.

Why then had they come? To report back perhaps — but to whom?

And as if this were not enough —
Yahweh to cope with.

MOURN WITH THE MOURNERS, EZEKIEL

My life,

a long susurration,
grief and outrage.

I am shunted about,
a dry weed in a wind,
my fool's cloak of moods
put on, put aside
random, calamitous.

Yahweh
shouts
through the air of my lungs,
as though tongue and throat and
articulation

were his, not my own —
the words not my own — and my own.

Despite reservations, I grant them entrance, this venerable troop.
And on the instant, unprecedented, awful.
Yahweh descended like a fiery blade unsheathed, stood between them and myself.
What rationale governed their intent?
It was never to be known.
How could it be known? Yahweh stood between.
Sword, scrim of pure light, explosion, thunderbolt.

It was as though in a gathering twilight, I was perusing a scroll. And without warning, lightning crossed the page.
A hand lay upon the text, a hand other than my own.
As though a finger paused above one word.
Marked it, with blood or fire.
What was the word?
Unknown. A mercy!
Peremptorily, a hand closed the scroll.

There stood between the elders and myself, the Presence, the Third.
Perhaps these leaders designed a simple exchange,
words, arguments, proposals concerning our people
woven across the loom of the hour?
Or was more at stake?
Whether or no, all was stilled, halted.
The Lord of time stood there.
Creation held its breath.

It was early spring.

Did a chill descend, was light withheld?
No flowers or trees unfolded, no birds sang.
A listening look came upon creation's face.
At the moment of shifting of tides, the seas stood still,
quivering like stallions at the starting gate.
Leviathan, plowing a furrow in the sea, halted in his tracks.
Among humans likewise: moneymakers, childbearers, pil-
grims, beggars, tycoons, tinkers and traders, sword makers and
plowmen, artificers and laborers.
Among those who slept, multitudinous dreams were stilled.
Gog and Magog, the predator giants, halted in midmotion.
Every thought and work stock still.
And what of the dead?
These were the image, the clue to that moment, and to the
One standing between.

◆ ◆ ◆

Peremptorily, Yahweh speaks, words of jealousy, wild love, fury,
intervention, threat, derision:

"Why so these ponderous satraps seek you out, Ezekiel!
What impulse drives them to your door —
interference, suborning, spying!
I will not hearken to them; neither will you.
Their hearts are airless closets, given over to darkness.
They have other gods than me.

"Their intent is hereby nullified.
Have no part with them who have no part with me.
They seek, forsooth, a credential — through you, whose only
credential is myself.
Behold, I stop their tongues; perhaps their ears will open at last.
Tell them this:
'Topple your idols. Return to me.'
Then drive them from your door." (14:1ff.)

THE USELESS VINE
Ezekiel 15

"Go, mortal one, into the forest.
Take in hand a sharp bolo.
Chop, slash,

pull down a long rope of vine,
a thick convolvulus.
Loosen its grip,
this throttling parasite.

"Treat it with care,
with gloved hands —
it reeks of poison.
Pull, tug, this side, that,
away and down,
free the burdened tree.

"Drag the serpentine rope
coiled and clinging
over ground and undergrowth —
a clearing.

"Appraise it now.
Are you a wood carver?
Do your eyes light up,
an artisan, a peerless block?
A nothing,
fetid stink of the vine!

"Or a householder,
seeking fuel for the fire?
Useless vine, wormwood,
runnel of bitter juices!

"Perhaps your search is simpler —
a peg to hang a garment?

"Twisting, coiling, perverse —
in a hundred length
no inch of sound wood!
Tell them —
poisonous, sterile vine,
clinging, suffocating
the great tree of creation!

"Woe to them.
With ax and bolo —
tear down, cast away!

"Useless, nefarious, noxious ones.
The end nears." (15:1ff.)

◆ ◆ ◆

A harsh variation on an ancient theme.

The vine of Ezekiel grows in no fruitful vineyard.

The parable summons to memory the bitter verses of the Song of Moses (Deut. 32:32), referring notably, not to the covenantal tribe, but to "the nations":

> Their enemies, corrupt as Sodom and Gomorra,
> are like vines that bear bitter and poisonous grapes,
> like wine made from the venom of snakes.

◆ ◆ ◆

Isaiah (5:1–7) takes up the theme in some detail.

His vineyard has received loving care. A sunny hillside was chosen, the soil carefully turned up, cleared of stones. Promising vines were planted, a watchtower built, a pit dug for treading the harvest.

All in vain. The grapes are sour as gall!

In consequence, the Vintner reverses every detail of care. Let weeds run riot, let briars and thorns prevail, wild beasts raven! For

> God awaited innocence and behold, bloodshed.
> God awaited justice and behold, the cry of victims!

◆ ◆ ◆

Jeremiah (2:21) echoes the plaint succinctly:

> I planted you like a choice vine
> from the very best seed.
> But look what you have become!
> A rotten worthless vine.

◆ ◆ ◆

Psalm 80 offers a like imagery, but with a difference. Now it is the enemies who enter and trample the vineyard, "the grapevine out of Egypt."

For a time, the "vine" flourished stupendously; it grew and stretched and throve, wildly surpassing its own metaphor.

An imperial "vine" this, producing an ambrosia worthy of Avignon. Look you. It "extended its branches to the Mediterranean Sea, as far as the Euphrates!"

Then, ruin. And according to the mournful harping of the Psalmist, all unmerited. The theme is of an innocence whelmed in catastrophe, all the more terrible for being willed by Yahweh:

> Why did you break down the fences around?...
> Wild hogs trample it down, wild animals feed on it.

◆ ◆ ◆

Only a hint here of the bitter theme of Ezekiel and the others; evil-doing has earned the fury of Yahweh. But something more — remorse: "We will never turn away from you again...."

A WOMAN TO BLAME
Ezekiel 16

A truly dreadful parable follows:

Yahweh: "Mortal one, tell them this story.
From birth and before, my people were — outsiders. No one, least of all yourselves, knew your parentage. Or cared greatly. You were
a tiny girl-child, newly born.
You were thrust into the world, unwanted.
Who would come forward to claim the newborn?
Whoever they were, mother, father, abandoned you.
No one to sever the cord, to cleanse or clothe you.
No pity, no love; you lay there barely alive, a foundling.

"I passed; I saw you, mewing in blood and filth.
Could I turn away?
Or am I a Samaritan god?
You must not die, I cried!
Mouth against mouth, I willed you back to life.
So you grew, wild, untamable, naked and fierce.
In time, a woman-child.

"Secretly my love grew.
None surpassing this beauty — your breasts, your hair, the scent of you!
It was the springtime of love.
I came to your side, and departed no more.
I spread a mantle over your beauty.
It was a kind of airy claim, and final.
I entered your body, even as you my soul.
There in the desert we wrought the marriage of heaven and earth.

"Did you grow tame, even as you taught me wild ways?
From the abundance of my trove, I clothed you, my beloved.

An embroidered gown, shoes of soft leather, a gold headband, and over all, a cloak of finest silk.

For you the treasures of Araby are foil — bracelets, necklace, earrings, and crowning all, a coronet.

Thence to the marriage banquet!

"Alas! That you could wreak havoc of our enchantment!

Troth plighted, the goblet raised, the marriage bed scented, we two sweetly entwined —

that night you crept forth from our couch.

You wandered the streets, bargaining like a strumpet, bedding with whatever scullion or slit-purse.

The infamy!

Gowns and jewels you handed over — to lovers as lubricious as yourself.

Once again, as in your childhood, you roved about naked and wild and squalid.

No child now, but a whore, peddling your wares in the public street!" (16:1ff.)

♦ ♦ ♦

One ponders such imagery with many a second thought, a heavy heart. Memories of Hosea bowing before a male deity, the malaise, the hatred and contempt of women — such images can hardly be termed helpful, or fragrant with good feeling.

♦ ♦ ♦

I have suggested elsewhere an exercise of "reversal of images."

The effort is painful and helpful at once. It implies the willingness to undergo, at least in prospective imagery, a reversal of roles and fortune.

♦ ♦ ♦

In this episode, let us see what comes of it.

Suppose: a female deity and her female prophet discover the infidelity of a male spouse.

Suppose moreover (as in the latter part of 16:26–29) the story takes on a wider import. The lubricious spouse is considered also as a symbol.

The symbol is enlarged.

The malaise of one human serves to illumine a veritable plague, a social disaster.

The holy One is aghast, divine hope is violated.

Now it is the male spouse who "lets your lustful neighbors, the Egyptians, go to bed with you."

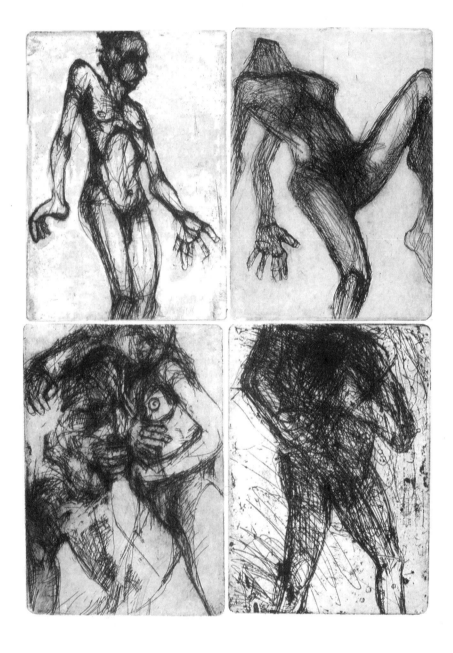

More: "I have handed you over to the Philistines, who know only disgust at your infamous conduct."

And yet more: a roving eye "runs after the Assyrians."

And finally, with a kind of delicious irony: "You were also a prostitute for the Babylonians, that nation of businessmen(!); no more did they satisfy you."

Thus the patrimony (*sic*) is squandered, in every detail and direction.

◆ ◆ ◆

At work in the parable is a strong, indeed unmistakable, supposition. It underlies the vertiginous splendor of the wedding imagery.

The setting is — Edenic.

The beauty of the bride and her habiliments, the jewels, the banqueting and rejoicing are splendidly excessive.

A coterie of gift-givers and handmaidens, the oriental world surrounds and crowns the bride.

◆ ◆ ◆

These are symbols of — grace, the bridal favor of covenant.

They signify gifts bestowed by a faithful tradition, long clung to, truthful, the embrace of reality, beneficent and transfiguring.

And it is all lost. Worse, flung away.

The parable is of surpassing irony and tragedy.

◆ ◆ ◆

Shall we consider another, far different outcome?

In other circumstances, this might well occur: reality, intuition, truth, tradition are cherished at all cost, even death.

We think of our own time, of the treasures guarded so closely by the suffering servants of Salvador, Guatemala, southern Africa.

◆ ◆ ◆

And how comes it that in a far different generation or time or culture, the tradition is scuttled, loses weight and significance and meaning?

And the loss occurs not only among the people at large, but among priests, bishops, preachers, popes?

◆ ◆ ◆

We have sorrowful examples all too close to hand.

Tradition: "the rock, *petros*," held firm for centuries. Call it stele, signpost, center, axis, pivot. People took soundings from it, and direction, and hope.

This rock was no blank slab, but a kind of Rosetta stone! A mysterious text overlaid its face, a calligraphy minute and exquisite: Gospels, prophetic oracles.

Also sacred symbols, signs, seven of them like cunning, hand-illumined letters, veritable presences.

The texts told of a long history of prayer, sustained by mystics and martyrs and virgins and confessors and common folk.

A long history also of heroism underscored in blood.

Art too had an honored place there, as the texts maintained — music and dance.

Evidence of tears stained the stone.

For centuries, multitudes undertook pilgrimages to the holy place. Only to put hand to the stone, to linger and weep there, in gratitude or grief or both.

◆ ◆ ◆

Is it simply that holy things are subject, like all human realities, to the erosion of time?

Or is there a lavic charge at the core of things, anger, resentment, exclusiveness, awaiting the moment of discharge?

We do not know.

◆ ◆ ◆

Of something however we do well to take note.

Beyond doubt the parable under consideration is dour, appalling, dispiriting.

It is also far and away the longest, most painfully detailed episode in Ezekiel.

Was it meant to be so? Is he implying, relentlessly, that waywardness and treachery are endemic to humans, forms of the sin we name "original"?

◆ ◆ ◆

And yet Ezekiel, for all the cold eye he casts on our plight, refuses to close his oracles on a basso profundo, beyond hope.

An astonishing breakthrough occurs, a reversal. A "despite all."

Is he himself the occasion of that grace, breakthrough, reversal?

Occasion and more — cause?

◆ ◆ ◆

Perhaps here one is permitted to generalize.

May one not assume that the lives and deaths of prophets like Ezekiel, the long line of holy women and men to our own day — these hardy, fractious ecstatics and lawgivers and truth-tellers — offer the strongest clue?

Can it be that because of them, Yahweh's worst moods (and our worst crimes!) do not prevail, do not bring creation to ruin?

♦ ♦ ♦

Despite all, the holy ones intercede and prevail. And two blessings follow.

First, a "forgetting of all," a casting aside of the will toward "quid pro quo" on the part of Yahweh.

No demands are laid down; nothing is heard of the ancient insistence on repentance and return.

♦ ♦ ♦

Friendship is simply restored — and this by free act of the offended party.

The theme of God's joyous initiative resounds through the centuries; "God has first loved us." "It is I who will once more make firm my alliance with you...."

♦ ♦ ♦

Thus a noble power is born in us.

Goodness divine creates human goodness, where only infidelity and despair and delinquency had reigned.

"On your part, you will remember your behavior, be seized with shame and reduced to silence."

This is the triumph of God — that our humanity be healed at last.

THE EAGLE AND THE VINE
Ezekiel 17

"Mortal one, a parable —
a great sky-ranging bird,
surpassing in beauty and majesty —
his wings owned the heavens;
his shadow lay large on the land.

"One day he flew and flew,
far, far as the horizon, beyond —
finally, wings folding,
he descended,
came to rest
in the swaying summit
of a gigantic cedar.

"There he stood, majestic.
It was as though
he held a levee on that throne.

His gaze ranged the horizon,
the look of an emperor of upper air.

"After a long time,
off again he flew
far O far —
straight into the eye of night.

"He took soundings from the stars,
then like an arrow from on high,
shot to earth.

"Cannily, exactly, easefully,
as though darkness were high noon,
he plucked a young vine,
root and all, from its ground.
Carefully, tenderly,
the slight burden
he bore homeward.

"Toward dawn,
heavy, weary,
he came to rest,
by dint of beak and claw,
planted the slender cutting in new soil.

"How the vine flourished!
leaves, harvest
yearning upward
toward his majesty,
ranging the skies,
hovering nearby,
guarding, surveying, keeping watch." (17:1–6)

◆ ◆ ◆

Yahweh: "Mortal one, tell of that cedar
which in my parable enthroned the eagle.
Tell my purpose.
Despite all, despite all! —
    The topmost branch,
    which sovereign Aquila
    graced with his presence —
I will pluck it away.

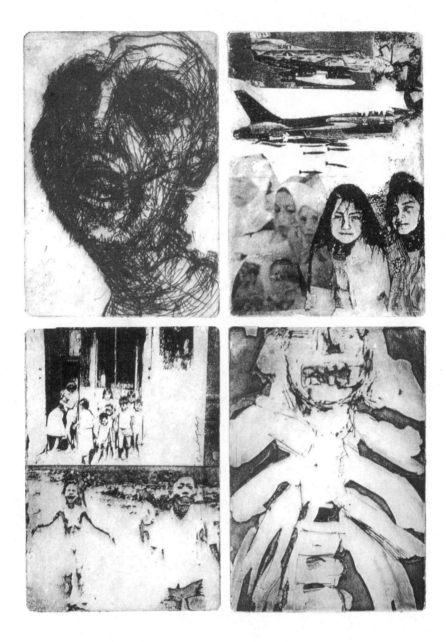

"Yes, that very branch.
(I too range far and wide;
  I too command air, sky, earth.)

"I shall take wing like an eagle. From end
to end of earth
    I bear the cedar bough,
    plant it anew —
    under my provenance
    how it shall flourish!

"Tell them of greatness to come!
High, unsurpassed,
that pillar of heaven,
haven for the birds of creation!

    "My tree, loud with birdsong,
a rainbow of light —
itself a splendid
bird of paradise!" (17:22–24)

◆ ◆ ◆

An oracle in two parts. The first, as envisioned here, a story of Yahweh Aquila, told by himself. The second, a story of what wonders
Yahweh will work, together with, on behalf of, even in despite of, this
unprepossessing tribe of ours.

◆ ◆ ◆

The sublime Eagle wearies, at times grows furious, jealous, recriminatory.
  We and our tainted lineage — What is to be done with us?
  The mighty experiment of Genesis, it would seem at times, has issued
in plain disaster.
  By day, year, generation, and aeon, individuals, entire cultures and
nations take up a vile, ever worsening burden — they widen, deepen,
heighten the scope of moral catastrophe.

◆ ◆ ◆

And yet, and yet, despite all — there is no giving up on us, no final
condemnation.
  Like a heave of birth, with groans and tears, this God swears an oath.
  Taking counsel with his heart, taking all in account, in no detail ignorant of our bloodshot biography — nonetheless God's holiness will not
be held hostage to wickedness.

◆ ◆ ◆

It is not for us (though so desiring, like a race of Jonahs) to dictate the beat and pace of God's heart.

Not for us — destitute as we are in virtue, inept, morally insipid — to set the scope of that mercy.

Despite all, despite the gods who pollute our hearts, God will be God.

AND WHO SHALL BE RESPONSIBLE?
Ezekiel 18

The famous breakthrough occurs to Ezekiel — and yet another bone of contention sticks in the throats of scholars and rabbis.

They much prefer, it would seem, the Mosaic law, with its insistence on generational guilt, the sins of the fathers visited on the sons.

Ezekiel will have nothing of this (as will Jesus: nothing.)

◆ ◆ ◆

Yahweh: "What is this proverb I hear bandied about —
  'The father ate sour grapes;
  the teeth of children are on edge' "?

"Foolish," Yahweh thundered. "No more of that!
This is what I demand of you, every one —
No hidden idolatries.
No lusting after a woman pledged.
No cheating, lying, stealing.
No oppression of others.
No usury.

"Rather this:
Feed the hungry;
clothe the naked.
Purpose no evil act;
render just judgment.
In behavior and speech
act in accord with the truth.

"Each of you is responsible before me.
For the sin of another,
no one will be called to account,
neither father nor son, mother nor daughter.
Thus my will and command.

"Do you think, perhaps, you so righteous ones, you coven of recalcitrants, that I take pleasure in the destruction of the wicked? that I choose to crush rather than raise up?

You think, perhaps, I resemble you?

If I resembled you, and the gods who so resemble you, I would long ago have brought down on your heads the pillars of creation.

No, I resemble you in no wise.

I am high noon to your blear night.

"Why then this pursuit of death, this recriminatory will?

Death, I confess with groaning, is a horror to me.

Take to yourselves my heart and spirit.

Be converted, and live." (18:1–32)

TWO SONGS
Ezekiel 19

THE LIONS, YOUR MOTHER
(A Poem Apt for the Exile)

Said to me: "Raise a song of grieving!

"A song of lions,
a lioness and her cubs!
The mother sleepless,
her eye a ring of fire,
unblinking, circling
the predatory dark!

"The cub resembles its sire,
ravening, man-eating,
the mountains reverberant
with rumble and roar!

"Alas for all that —
ruin stalks the mighty;
behold the gold-maned princeling —
shamed and shorn
cast to ground, shrouded in nets,
tangled there raging, then
subdued, obeisant —
spirit broken

under the tamer's whip
caged
among gawking humans
for circuses and show!" (19:1–9)

THE VINE THAT COULD NOT
(A Second Song of Grief)

"A vine
hardy, noble,
firm planted,
mother of all —
prospering, bearing its
harvest and plunder.

"Arbor overarching,
womb of sweet repose
wherein lingered languid
and played betimes
sun shaft, shadow,
'green thought in a green shade.'

"And O her fruit, that
teeming clustering
weight of glory!
            as though
each globule
an egg of the universe,
smooth as Eve's brow,
cracked.
            And lo!
birth, rebirth
Our Easter,
unimaginable —
            bones like sticks
in tarry dip, stood fiery!

"Lo, her wine in us, vine
in us
            arterial tracery —
a mother's hand
held us
            newborn, red

as sunset's roses
        up and up
for all the world: See!

"See —
     shame.
       Sons, wreckers
      pull down that glory,
        brown, charred,
        sere, a shroud.

"A dry sigh
       powdery leaves
utter into the dry
sigh of desert winds,
          alas!
       and again
       alas!

"A burning droplet,
      tear or sap
   mid the scouring flames,
stands, brief.
Saw it you, or not!"

      God,
      pressing,
      grief. (19:10–14)

◆ ◆ ◆

Strange as may seem to ourselves, these "passing songs" of grief seem to have been composed for relief and recovery.

Cries in face of a rousing culture that seems to know only emotions opposite to grief, celebrating a strictly mythic, self-aggrandizing past. And in the present too, military conquest, invasions, spurious victories.

No. Grieve.

◆ ◆ ◆

Here and there in our day too, and rarely, one comes on such as Ezekiel and his confreres. These raise in their hearts, if not in public, such dirges as here dim our eyes.

It is as though the tears of those who grieve, then and now, were dramatizing the tears of Yahweh, overflowing into history.

◆ ◆ ◆

One knows a few things. Others do not — or choose not to.

The claim is hardly a matter of declaring moral superiority. Rather something of simple honesty.

(How did Camus put it? He did not seek a world in which murder is not committed. He was more modest: he sought a world in which murder is not justified.)

◆ ◆ ◆

A few cry murder, cry violence and duplicity on high.

Others, for whatever reason, are mute.

Most rush to the ramparts of the status quo. In private or public, they make casuistic or jingoistic sense of — murder.

◆ ◆ ◆

The authorities are another matter entirely.

They see no blood on the flag, admit to no dishonor, whether to conscience or Bible or constitution or bill of rights or international law.

Which is to say, the lawless are a law unto themselves.

In face of repeated wars and incursions, in contempt for the poor, in despisal of the law of God (or the law of the land!), they see nothing to renounce or contemn.

Thus does a certain brand of "power and might" inhibit truthful understanding of crime and consequence.

◆ ◆ ◆

Surely we are called in such circumstance to play Ezekiel.

To mourn in our hearts, to mourn in public: in places of worship, in overt public acts of civil disobedience.

We mourn for the crimes adduced; also (as in the oracles of Ezekiel), for the retribution to come.

◆ ◆ ◆

Such mourners know something, and the knowledge is both a torment and a spur.

To wit: the gods who drive the world's engine are blind.

And they strike their votaries blind, an epidemic that then seizes on the multitudes.

The illness can only be described clumsily; call it "inconsequentiality."

Which is to say, crime has no consequence, no judgment attached. Strike and run free.

◆ ◆ ◆

Indeed, as many insist heatedly, to attach the word "crime" to this or that event (wars, executions, assisted suicides, abortions, racist perdurances) is to place in contention a sensible logical issue (women's rights, vindication of domestic law and order, "national interests").

Thus, to make of an expedient lesser evil a crime, is to poison the air. Or so it is adduced.

The mourners, on the other hand, hold (and closely guard) a different "worldview."

But perhaps not so different from an angle of vision commended by the Bible.

MEMORY IS A HARSH, HEALING PRESENCE
Ezekiel 20

Something momentous is at hand; the day, month, and year are duly noted.

In exile, certain among the elders and princes and priests approach Ezekiel. They could hardly be thought of as votaries of the troublesome prophet. Their motives in arriving at his door remain unclear.

Or perhaps, in view of the quick, all-but-savage intervention from on high, nullifying their purpose on the moment — perhaps their motives are all too clear. At least to Yahweh.

They are set back, rebuked, silenced by a far different, fiercely intrusive agenda. Excoriation, denunciation!

◆ ◆ ◆

These notables, one concludes, have much of fear and little of affection toward Ezekiel.

Time and again they have been excoriated by a "word of Yahweh," issued in despite of (almost in despisal of) their pride of place. A word scalding to the souls of the religious imperialists.

Undoubtedly these witnessed his public mimes, also directed at their eminences — and seldom in flattering fashion.

Nonetheless, the worst has befallen — as he predicted in season and out. So it might well be to their advantage to take soundings — even from a madman.

The prudence of the mighty dies hard. From time to time the elders find it to their sorry advantage (he was, all said, correct in his prognostications: the exile is a brutal fact) to enter the dwelling of the prophet and converse with him.

◆ ◆ ◆

The lust for worldly advantage perdures, despite all.

They enter, listen, debate. And all to what advantage? What reception do they accord his oracles? What submission to God's word follows on the hearing?

We are told nothing.

Perhaps there is nothing to tell. What authority remains to them? Is envy the driving force here? What authority, by reason of prophecy and fulfillment (even the bitter fulfillment of exile), has accrued to the prophet?

These "leaders of the community," as Ezekiel refers to them somewhat laconically, tread the pages of our book, shadowy figures in the twilit existence of exile. In striking contrast, be it noted, to the prophet's burning moral presence. "They shall know that a prophet stands in their midst." Indeed.

Take it or leave. A nay-sayer he, and a yea-sayer; and each monosyllable lucid, beyond misapprehending.

◆ ◆ ◆

And they? The delegation stands before Ezekiel, as though in a moral crepuscule, a blur.

What was their complicity in the crimes that led to the exile? Were they among the adherents of the temple idolatry that brought the nation down?

Now, in exile, the question will not die: Where do they stand? Whether in behavior or word, they refuse to declare themselves — whether vis-à-vis the tyrant who holds their people in thrall, or the will of Yahweh, or (as must follow) the teaching of Ezekiel.

One is led to a suspicion: they may well be a species of collaborator; whether by silence or overt action, they are aligned with the worldly powers, assimilated, slavish of spirit.

◆ ◆ ◆

They can hardly be imagined composing or singing the preceding dirges. Such songs reverberate only on the tongues of — the faithful, the remnant, the resisters.

◆ ◆ ◆

Doom in the offing, doom in effect!

The sequel, here as in chapter 14, is a word of interruptive catastrophe. On neither occasion will Yahweh squander a moment on the concerns, however imagined, of the elders. Their authority is null and void. Their sins have brought the nation down.

So the initiative is simply snatched from them.

◆ ◆ ◆

A different agenda! The prophet is instructed brusquely to announce an event that, strangely enough, has already come to pass: the downfall of the nation.

Strange; they sit in exile — and the destruction of the holy city and the driving forth are announced as imminent.

A strange warp of time.

But perhaps not so strange after all. This Yahweh is a great instructor of the morally obtuse, ourselves. The connections above all! Lost to sight and mind in the Fall, these must constantly be reconstituted, a second creation of the soul.

Sin and consequence, yin and yang!

The force of the present misery, the destruction of all that was dear and valued, is so overwhelming that its cause is accepted, and then forgotten. One loses the past, its meaning and drive, the impelling cause, the infection — the temple outrages, the injustices. Crime and consequence.

Dig it up, expose it to view! Thus to unmask a prevailing myth, one that was daily celebrated in a thousand ways, from market to palace to sanctuary to armed forces: the myth of diurnal national prospering.

The myth of crime — and no consequence.

◆ ◆ ◆

Thus the dirges of Ezekiel, their images standing over against the boasts and toasts, the flaunting of flags, the overweening rhetoric of civic virtue, the parades of national grandezza.

Nothing of these, you fools. You were fools in prosperity; you remain such in lands afar, stripped to the bone.

Memories of empire deceive, distract. Mourn rather, grieve, turn away, fast and keep watch, weep bitter tears.

There is a confession of guilt to be exacted.

For there is a God.

◆ ◆ ◆

The mournful chant of Ezekiel, how bracing! The themes of ruin, desolation, downfall, the smoking fag end of empire. Accept, admit!

Saving, bracing the song. Also grumbling, truculent, the cries of a born disturber of the peace.

The crimes of the nation are ubiquitous, he insists. They are visible to all but the perpetrators — the international fomenting of violence, the domestic injustice.

The end is at hand; downfall is imminent. (Imminent? Accomplished, a fact. Downfall has — fallen.)

◆ ◆ ◆

This is the rub. Even in reverie, the elders will tolerate a word of superficial reform (a subject in which Ezekiel is totally uninterested, whether it falls to the temple priesthood or the system at large).

He insists, stakes life and limb on this: the prophetic word is a political word. The fait accompli has a powerful charge; the exile could well be the seedbed of a new start. For, if the victims will grow reflective, their fallen estate strikes at the heart of the "system," unmasks public crime, summons those responsible for the disaster, to judgment. Unpalatable, discomfiting!

◆ ◆ ◆

That truth of things, how rarely come by in our day!

It amounts to little more than a Rorschach test, administered to children.

What do you see of reality?

Make of it what one will, anyone's guess, surmise, hunch...

And then the monstrous impediments. We are offered blots of ink, sound bites, promises promises, political hacks squaring off noisily, winner and loser alike devoid of substance and will, images of the media — mediating only illusion.

"I see men like trees, walking."

CRIME AND CONSEQUENCE
(As a Recall of Chapter 14)

Well I remember,
driven like nails in flesh;
seven nails, seven years —
exile, fifth month, tenth day.

Arrived a delegation,
gray beards all.
Due solemnity, nidnodding unison —
"concerning the Lord's will."

More than they bargained for!
Could they
in worst dream
conjure the fierce
torrential incursion,
the thunderous monologue
riving their solemn assembly!

That day, no
"discourse of civility,"
jawbones nattering
this nostrum or that,

a stench of cold comfort
corpse on corpse bestowing.

"NO! HEAR MY WORD
CONCERNING CRIME AND CONSEQUENCE!"

A voice cries aloud
on the affrighted air —
no comfort, none.

The Lightning Wielder
loots with a stroke
the vessel of memory, reality.

Backward, forward,
uncontrollable sweeping
as wheat fields in a gale —

in blood or fire;
a hand writes —

"MY WORD
CONCERNING CRIMES ACCOUNTABLE." (20:1ff.)

◆ ◆ ◆

It is an old story, and an ironic one, constantly summoned by the prophets — a story of betrayal and liberation.

The Yahweh of Ezekiel might be thought of as a cosmic memory, an immense scroll encircling, recording, taking careful note of creation and time, encompassing history and ethic, lapses and fidelities, prescribed worship and covenantal law.

From first day of Genesis to thunderous summing up of Revelation, all is held firm, recorded in hand and heart, all remembered.

◆ ◆ ◆

In our passage the Memory mightily concentrates on one section, one phrase even of that all-encompassing prescience.

My mercy, your reneging.

◆ ◆ ◆

We humans. Including by implication the elders here, we are great ones for — selective forgetting.

A convenient ploy, a willed erasure of scene and occasion — and we walk unscathed away from this or that crime: air war, land war, capital execution, throttling sanctions.

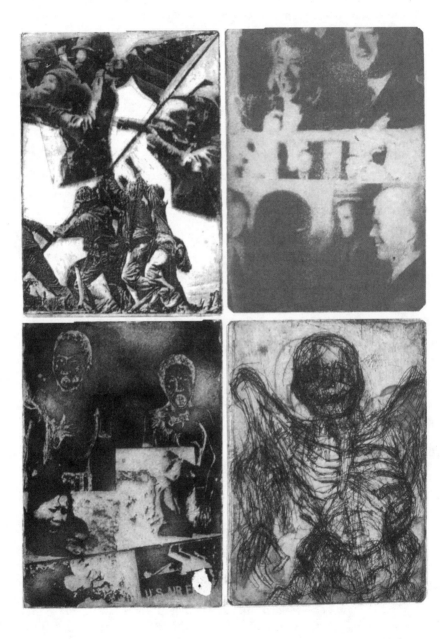

Thus the history of our culture tells of a rake's passage through time, marked and marred by the debris of responsibilities discarded, dismissed, crimes unconfessed, victims unrequited.

We much prefer to function under the illusion, perpetually invoked, of something known as a "fresh start."

If only we can "put this or that behind us"!

◆ ◆ ◆

But "this or that," whether a war, a murder, a betrayal (these scarcely ever named for what they are, a tawdry euphemism instead) — these are canny ghosts indeed, and continue to dog us.

This dog might be thought a lead dog, trained on behalf of the blind. At some point, the dog literally takes the lead. For we are in principle blind.

◆ ◆ ◆

Another image.

Such amnesia as afflicts us, when elevated to a personal and social virtue, is a kind of wrecking ball swung against culture and covenant, against our very humanity.

The signs, the cracks, are visible, without and within.

The wanton blows, repeated again and again, will bring us down.

◆ ◆ ◆

As to the elders and Ezekiel. Presumably they sought him out in the name of their (and his) people, the exiles.

What they expected to hear, what topics they purposed raising, what word of Yahweh they awaited, perhaps to report back to the afflicted community (or perhaps to the oppressors?) — of these matters we can only speculate.

Of their intentions, interests, concerns, curiosity of mind, sense of the occasion, we learn precisely nothing.

◆ ◆ ◆

Had they intended to question God, to raise a plaint of Job, as to why affliction had been visited on the chosen ones?

Or had they in mind to reprove God, to debate the prophet and his doomsday proclivities, to argue against him their communal or personal innocence?

Or did they seek to learn the hour of liberation, or what place they might attain in the new order of things following on the great return? Or perhaps they had in mind to turn the occasion to a kangaroo court, indicting the prophet?

◆ ◆ ◆

Not one of these concerns is raised. A spin, a turnabout!

On the moment it is their lives, their motives and appetites and egos, that are radically placed in question. Naked they stand.

Worldly wisdom in contention with divine. No contest!

Their plans, speculations, proposals, are aborted.

◆ ◆ ◆

They enter the room, and are struck mute on the instant.

In Jerusalem, did they not have the upper hand, for generations, the initiative, the authority? Was not the word of Yahweh their charge and glory?

Their mouths are stopped, their words swept away in a gale.

Everything come to naught. It is as though they had not ventured on the errand at all.

◆ ◆ ◆

Has God read those hearts, and found them — wanting?

No introductions, no courtesies. Abrupt, provocative, insulting.

Their situation is radically altered, as by a literal Act of God.

A mysterious Other intervenes. They stand before Ezekiel under a new aegis and agenda — his.

◆ ◆ ◆

What a scene! No dialogue here, such as is reported between Job, Moses, Jeremiah, Ezekiel himself — and Yahweh.

Only thunderous reproof and rebuke. The presumption of the visitors is cast back at them. "Have you come here to consult with Me? As I live, I will not be consulted by the likes of you."

The implication is indubitable. Consultation with Ezekiel is equivalently consultation with Yahweh. No clearer credential could be imagined or offered.

◆ ◆ ◆

Yahweh then introduces an agenda vastly at odds with that of the visitors.

Something terrible is introduced: judgment. "Are you, Ezekiel, prepared to judge them? Then do so."

◆ ◆ ◆

The words that follow are wrought in the furnace of divine fury. Yahweh reads the texts of these hearts; what He finds there is beyond doubt evidentiary.

They have lived and continue to live, not by covenant, but by an abominable antiscripture:

"Crimes...seductive horrors...soiled with idolatry...rebels...profaners...prostitutes..."

Likewise, words of retribution, delayed perhaps but always impending: "Massacre...exterminate..."

◆ ◆ ◆

We note an all but unbearable irony.

These are the appointed spiritual leaders of the people. More, they, along with the people, are enduring a harsh exile.

Far from the image of Daniel and the faithful remnant, these leaders set about aping the moral code of their captors, even while they pretend to a life of fidelity.

What lies buried in those hearts? What beneath the conventional gestures of fealty and faith drives such lives?

In the precincts of the Jerusalem temple, they were in servitude to other gods. The slavery continues under a distant sun.

◆ ◆ ◆

Yahweh reads aloud, with crushing irony, the text they would fain conceal: "As for the dream that haunts your spirit — I hear you say in your hearts, 'We wish to ape the nations, to bow down to sticks and stones!' — I assure you this will never come to pass."

◆ ◆ ◆

It is ourselves, all said, who are indicted here.

The dream of assimilation to the empire, a dream soiled and despoiling, seldom admitted to, never entirely put to rout — is our own dream. The sin of origins, made "original" once more.

◆ ◆ ◆

What depths we would fall to, what demons give ourselves to, apart from grace! apart from the firm unyielding embrace that holds us — despite the gravitational pull of the culture — giddily, even unwillingly upright.

◆ ◆ ◆

Judgment, in scalding detail.

And finally a promise: an end to the collective amnesia of the distempered delegates; a grace, conversion of heart: "Then at length you will remember your disgraceful acts, your self-soiling...."

◆ ◆ ◆

Surely, if the secret will of the elders were honored here, there would survive no record of the humiliation that descended on them, swept them and their plans aside; all but swept them off the earth, a debris.

Abasement, spleen, chagrin is their portion.
We imagine their shamed departure.
Not a word.

What record of the event we have is offered by Ezekiel and his like, at long last and for once vindicated.

That truth of his was long despised and put to naught by the machinations of the great. They sat the saddle of history; he all but perished under the hooves of the four horsemen.

And how the mighty have come to naught, how altered are roles, authorities, principalities!

The downfall of the nation was also an epiphany of the truth.

The one who went unheard for years, whose mimes were accounted the confabulations of a madman, whose tale of disaster impending was dismissed out of hand — now, now, now we shall see!

This Yahweh is a very maestro of the music of the spheres.

Play on, Ezekiel, play on! — themes of conjunctions to come, mutualities delayed, rings of light revealed, long patience and its rewards.

JUDGMENT: YAHWEH CHANGES SIDES
Ezekiel 21

LOOK TO IT: THE SWORD OF THE SPIRIT

Spoke to me thus:
"Mortal one, I am the groan in your guts,
the fear that stops your heart,
      the helpless hands,
      the open vein, the courage
draining away,
      the knees turned to water.

"You say to me, protesting:
Do not send me to this people,
their mickmocking —
      'Behold the perverse one!
He takes delight
in blank riddles!'

"For them, mortal one, this:
the sword is ready. Look,
I myself place it,
      close it tight,

as lover's hand in lover's —
Mine, Yours!

"Unmerciful Cossack —
scream like a hellion!
Strike left, strike right,
        a Saturn, a circle of fire!

"The edge
is laid to the throat.
One thrust, and quietus —
foul rejoicing
ends in a bloody welter.

"Strike then!
        On that day
        (My Day and yours!)
the princes tumble like ninepins,
the palace a house of cards,
crowns, scepters — loot
of the smile and sack of time.

"Then, then, My Day —
        Lazarus sits to banquet,
        the mighty householders, scored and sore,
languish like dogs at the gate." (21:1ff.)

◆ ◆ ◆

The theme is familiar: reversal of fortune, subversion of the ways and means of the mighty.

And this, be it noted, in the heyday of Jerusalem, even as the world's ways tempt (worse — win over) the chosen and their would-be spokesmen.

◆ ◆ ◆

Like a curved scimitar, the oracle bends and twists with surprise. Astonishingly, pagans are enlisted to bring the "just" to judgment.

◆ ◆ ◆

Ezekiel 21:23–32. The scene shifts. Now the sword is placed in other hands, that of the invader.

In preparation for the battle of Jerusalem (and in prospect of victory), we are told how the gentile warriors undertake certain methods of divination.

Elsewhere, performed by the chosen, such practices have been condemned as revolting, idolatrous.

Yet here, King Nebuchadnezzar prepares with magic rites to launch his assault on the holy city.

And no judgment is laid against his behavior. We are offered only a straightforward account of the proceedings.

◆ ◆ ◆

The mighty invaders stand at a crossroads. Against whom shall they move?

The king "draws forth the marked arrows, consults the teraphim, examines the liver of an animal."

Then the decision: the assault is to proceed.

◆ ◆ ◆

The story of the "crossroads," the army poised, the next move uncertain, the magic rites — these become the elements of an extraordinary parable. It is not only Nebuchadnezzar who stands at the threshold of an awesome choice.

It is the people of Jerusalem.

And according to the plain sense of the imagery, they have already chosen. They have chosen badly.

No question here, whether of condoning or condemning pagan practices. Nor is the scene to be thought a gesture of contempt, tossed in the direction of insuperably ignorant outsiders.

◆ ◆ ◆

More is surely at stake. A woeful logic governs the pagan rite and its aftermath.

Idolatry on the part of the invaders becomes a kind of maleficent pointing finger, an instrument of judgment — against the idolatry of the chosen.

Thus the magical rite becomes a mirror, a reproach, a truth made visible.

◆ ◆ ◆

The hand that honors the idols is the hand of a pagan king; this is a reality, a rite. But it is also an image held high, a countersign to the "In Hoc Signum Vinces."

The hand that holds the sign aloft for all to see (or to turn away from, in cowardice or terror) is the hand of God.

He speaks, in judgment.

A judgment against the chosen: "The visions you summon are false, the prophecies lies."

❖ ❖ ❖

No such word, be it noted, is spoken against the imperial outsiders.
They worship their gods, move with speed and dispatch. And prevail.

❖ ❖ ❖

And in a crushing reversal, Yahweh has turned and turned about.
Somewhere in the background of the scene, He hovers, changes sides.
Now He is "with them." He takes his stand with the pagans.
His decree: let the siege proceed; idols at war with idols.
Myth against myth.
No more standing with His own.
God — in this bitter instance — withstanding them.

ABOMINATIONS, CONSEQUENCE
Ezekiel 22

Said to me Yahweh: "Mortal one, make known the crimes of the City of Blood.

Say to them: Your end approaches. Guilt has set the clocks to the verge of midnight.

The hour nears. Creation holds its breath.

"The death you inflict on others has become your debit. In the geography of centuries and nations, the debt stands high as a Himalaya.

The nations despise you, even as you sedulously ape them — in murder, deceit, violence of every sort, in greed and usury, in dishonoring the elderly, in putting the needy to the door, in oppressing widow and orphan, in profaning my sabbath, in sexual perversity.

Your princes, your authorities, are murderers; they are lions and wolves, devouring their prey.

Like Shakespearean villains, they make bold to appear at the funeral of their victims, laying hand upon inheritances, even upon mourning widows.

"Your priests work profanations. They trample sabbath underfoot, muddying with casuistry the plain sense of the decalogue.

Your prophets whitewash the sepulchers of criminals. They mouth fervently: Thus ordains the Lord!

And all the while, I keep scornful silence.

"Every refinement of sin! even while the priests chatter on about 'moral grandeur,' 'chosen people,' 'covenant.'

Behold them, the world's laughingstock!

And the people untaught, steeped in ignorance, grow comatose; their spirit rots.

"Amid the welter of incoherence, I have sought and sought — someone; one just man, only one.

Someone to build a strong wall, to stand atop it, a guardian. To raise the alarm.

To cry: Yahweh approaches! Awaken!

"Tell them: Like chaff in a whirlwind, the people will be scattered abroad.

Tell them. The cause.

Because in soul and spirit, you are already scattered abroad, lost in a moral whirlwind. Am I to be dishonored forever?

Ask them.

If dishonor is my lot, let it come from the nations who know me not, rather than from you.

From you does it come! Therefore be scattered.

"Say this to their leaders: You are a useless metal, a 'massa damnata.'

Of silver or gold, nothing. A lavic flow of waste metal, base copper, tin, iron, lead. Everything precious eked out of you.

Tell them.

I thrust you — copper, tin, iron, lead, into a furnace.

I stoke the fury of my heart. Never have mortals endured such fires!

I shall meld and purify you, base metal, all." (22:1–22)

PARABLE OF THE SISTERS
Ezekiel 23

"Hear, mortal one, a parable.
I speak of a woman.
    And what to say of her, caught as I am between grief and anger?
      For awhile she called herself mine.
        She was no more mine than the sun,
      ranging the heavens, is yours.

She called herself mine,
    and all the while, played the whore.
She sought the beds of the elite,
the high officials of the land.
    Then at length,
        the heyday of her hedonism passed.
She and her children
discovered in the house of a paramour.
    Each and all, murdered.

    "Shortly
I set against your whoring — a great army in array.
    In the space of a horrid night
    ruin befalling,
        a thicket of shields, helmets, swords,
    chariots, siege works
    hemming you in.

    "Did you not cozen those warriors,
        seek after their giddy hearts?
Did they not purport to love you once,
        bedizen you, bed you?

    "They will rend you naked,
    seize you, bind you close, hail you into their courts.
They will invoke their laws, condemn and execute you.
    No one spared.
    Your children will die by fire.

"Mortal man, say to this people, once mine, mine no more:
You shall drink the cup of whoredom.
A cup wide, deep as an arroyo of hell.
A deluge!
The cup brims with gall — scorn and derision.
To the lees you will drink it — desolation, devastation." (23:1ff.)

◆ ◆ ◆

If we linger over the foregoing, it is only to be reminded of a crucial truth.

The imagery, here and elsewhere, is both pernicious and pervasive: an image of sexual deviation, the woman as evil; evil embodied in the female yielding to evil.

◆ ◆ ◆

Hosea developed the theme in painful detail (chapter 3): the momentous male bonding between Yahweh and prophet. The woman Gomer given over to evil, the personal stain enlarged to an image of social evil.

◆ ◆ ◆

The imagery is appalling. But few among the commentators are led to say so. (They, after all, being male, are among those whose image benefits from male divine-human bonding.)

And as to our prophets Hosea and Ezekiel: Are not their writings after all the "word of Yahweh"? And what more serendipitous credential?

◆ ◆ ◆

Inevitably, throughout the ages, questions have arisen among the devout who pondered those pages.

Who is in charge of this wondrous thing called creation?

Who brought it into being?

And all too shortly — Who brought it down, this encompassing tent of glory?

Who first "fell," and thereupon enticed the (not so intelligent) male into joining the cosmic free fall?

And so on and so on. From Genesis through Hosea, and unto our Yahweh-Ezekiel passage, the divine-human bond, a covenant within covenant, is renewed and strengthened.

Mutual stroking is all.

◆ ◆ ◆

Let it be granted at long last: assurances to the contrary notwithstanding, the covenantal bond as it touches on us humans includes as fully equal partners but half the race.

(As to the assurances to the contrary etc.: equal dignity is asserted straight-faced; but, of course, "no female priesthood.")

(The church as "animal farm": the language, duplicitous, straight-faced, is truly awesome. Assurance, possession, nine points of the law. "All pigs are equal, but some pigs are more equal than others.")

The woman stands apart, an outsider and worse. A figure of shame, an enticement, unchanged, unredeemed, the quintessential troublemaker.

◆ ◆ ◆

Thus once more in the Ezekiel episode, an ancient imagery is borrowed, sanctioned and set in place. With an added measure (one almost thinks, an added malice) of originality.

But in essence, regarding "the woman," our oracle much resembles the book of origins.

To wit: Eve and her daughters are sinners; more, they occasion the sin of others. In perpetuum.

DEATH BE THE SIGN
Ezekiel 24

THE DAY THE POT BOILED OVER

"Mortal one, mark well this day —
inscribe on a scroll
'the day of the pot-au-feu.'

"Mime this day. It is mine!
  Thus mark the day:
  a bronze cauldron
fill to brim —
thrust wood beneath, strike fire,
cast in the choicest meats,
set them brewing, boiling away.

"Toil and trouble and the bloodshot city!

"Torrents of blood
fall and fall!

"I cup my hands;
the blood of the innocent
pools there,
gathers greatly on itself —
blood will have blood!

"Cursed be the bloodshot city!
Behold me,
a butcher I arise!
hands, apron reeking blood!
Gather more wood.
Stoke the fire.
Boil the broth.
Burn bones to an ash!

"Then
set the cauldron
on residual coals —
corrosion burns off,

the bronze glows
purified a sun at zenith —

"No longer city of blood!
No longer cauldron of wrath!" (24:2–11)

◆ ◆ ◆

Who then is to burn, in our time and place?

The president retains the sanctions against Iraq. No medicine, no food. Children continue to die.

Against Cuba likewise.

◆ ◆ ◆

And do the churches protest?

They do not. The American Catholic bishops address the president, endorsing the "use of force" in Bosnia. A friend writes: "Thus they proclaim a peculiar view: that Jesus Christ would approve the death under smart bombs of civilians, caught in the fires of 'collateral damage.'"

◆ ◆ ◆

Gandhi, after Hiroshima: "It is fairly simple to count the cost of the atom bomb on the population of that city. It will require a longer time to assess the damage to the soul of the nation that dropped the bomb."

◆ ◆ ◆

The "longer time" has elapsed; the assessment is toted up.

The damage to the soul of the nation that dropped the bomb is clear, blindingly so. To all but the perpetrators and their advocates. These have launched our subsequent litany of crime and punishment — Vietnam, Grenada, Panama, Iraq.

Others will ponder the outcome. As God will judge.

WELL LOVED, ILL LOST

Said to me Yahweh: "Mortal one, you
my signature, my credential.

"Amanuensis, messenger you are.
Write this bold, clear, covenantal —
THUS SAYS YAHWEH
signed, sealed, delivered. My word.

"In the world, be my sign.
Dumb, deaf as a post, stand there.

Pointing, appointing,
in seasons vile and fair,
venturesome starts,
prognostications rare.

"This day, this awful day,
mark it well! —
I pluck the heart from your breast
　(nevertheless
　　that heart I hold in mine).

"Look, torn from your side,
your dearest helpmeet
first last love —
the delight of your eyes,
the desire of your soul.
But make no mourning for the dead.
Sigh, but not aloud. . . . "

Ezekiel: So I spoke to the people
in the morning,
and at evening
my wife died.
And on the next morning,
I did as I was commanded.

Yahweh: "Death be the sign."
　Stark, unmourned.
　Tears forbidden —
eyes
arid as desert stones.
No shroud. No bread of tears.
Nothing,
nor bitter nor sweet,
of courtesy or custom,
attend this passing.

"Only believe —
your heart's love,
your dearest countersign,
I hold in mine, a lesser
fire in immensity of fire.

"Distempered they question —
'Man of stone,

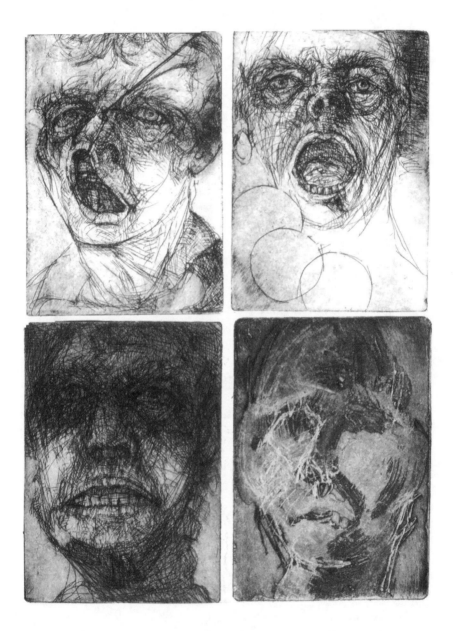

have gentler ways
fled the earth, that you
who once comported
with love's tender
consort, pivot, and plenary —
count this no loss at all,
she at dawn flourishing
at evensong vanished!'

"What they shall live to see!
and seeing entreat
the multitudinous harvester —
Come death, come, swift relief!

"Their stronghold,
their joy and glory
the delight of their eyes
and their heart's desire,
their sons and daughters,
tender in mien and frame —
all perished.
Death be the sign,
the dying unhouseled,
tears forbidden,
eyes
arid as desert stones.
No shroud. No bread of tears.
Nothing of courtesy or custom
attend this visitation, death's
angel, sword drawn against
first,
last born,
each and every." (24:15–27)

◆ ◆ ◆

Ezekiel is summoned.

Once more he is instructed to mime a coming event, to stand as a public sign.

We have seen it before, he has often undergone it.

It is his dignity and burden, the burden heavy, at times beyond all bearing. In such a world as ours, he must dramatize the will (and mood!) of the holy One. To point and say: this is of God.

But also: that is not of God; that is of the idols.

◆ ◆ ◆

Thus he becomes witness and signatory and warrant of the God who will not abandon the world, even as he chastises its wayward clan. Chastisement, harsh love!

Thus Ezekiel and his like interpret, render less unbearable, "God's most deep decree."

One almost said, God's "suffering-with."

◆ ◆ ◆

Such awful events he must announce!

The exile shortly to befall (then befallen), with all its accompanying indignities.

What must be, must be. He can in no wise alter the matter of the decree (which, in any case, has long since been enacted and exacted).

Still, he can do something, can help his people come through. Can insist that the catastrophe has meaning, consequence, is an occasion of eventual good.

Good, to come of this?

Come what may, they (and he) are not to give up, not to collapse in cynicism and despair.

◆ ◆ ◆

Time and again, as we have seen, he has been led to play the fool, in full public eye.

To mime the siege of Jerusalem and the sorry departure into exile. Then to lie, face to the ground, immobile, miming the long duration of exile.

To eat the scant rations of slavery, to illustrate deportation and death, and so on.

◆ ◆ ◆

We have pondered the harsh instruction as to the actions and their outcome. In course of his street theater, difficult and humiliating as it is, he is to remain detached from the reception, the response, the ears that hearken or set themselves itching, the thoughtful attendance or scornful turning away.

The outcome of his message, for good or ill, is nothing of his affair. The play's the thing.

They will know the truth, even in refusal of the truth.

◆ ◆ ◆

What detachment of heart, obedient clinging, purity of intent, concentration on essentials — what such work wrings from the soul, we have learned something of. For a lifetime.

◆ ◆ ◆

But in the present episode something far different, more ominous and awful is to be endured.

Death is now the sign. And how convey the reality, the catastrophe ever nearing?

◆ ◆ ◆

(How convey the "total war," the "collateral damage," the death of innocents, children, spouses, noncombatants [that former protected species, now in the eye of indifferent gun-sights]? How convey the horror, the blank loss, the children of the Balkans, of Somalia, the mothers of such as Stephen Biko or Bobby Sands?)

◆ ◆ ◆

How convey (closer perhaps to our issue) this: the laceration and loss attendant on American wars invariably fall on others than ourselves. The wars occur elsewhere; "elsewhere" becomes a kind of subconscious incantation of irresponsibility. Out of sight, out of mind's eye as well.

◆ ◆ ◆

But let it be said: the God of Ezekiel remains — God. The radius of that saving cordon of distance shortens, as the hour of retribution approaches.

The long memory of the holy One! The horrors, Ezekiel insists, come home to roost. They fall on a people who have long considered themselves immune from the fate they have subjected others to.

(Unprepared, unschooled as we are in suffering and loss; no, more, immune from these, as we persuade ourselves. Unprepared by reason of truth neglected, and a heavy overlay of besotted mythology.)

◆ ◆ ◆

The truth is — guilt. The overlay is — presumed innocence.

How convey the truth?

One way, a terrible one. The divine logic is relentless. Ezekiel himself must submit before — death.

This is a hard saying, hard as hell.

Death up close. In his own household, "the delight of your eye... taken away from you at a stroke."

Here is the rub; it rubs the soul raw.

◆ ◆ ◆

But what of those, we ask, who do not suffer, who walk unscathed through the gauntlet they have contrived?

The immune ones will bear close watching.

These godlings riding high and mighty in the world, technological lightning bolts in hand. Time after time they inflict heavy suffering on others.

They admit of no consequence, no guilt. They assume a guise of innocence, denigrating and demonizing the enemy.

◆ ◆ ◆

Thus continues the scenario of the Fall, an antiscripture whose chief authors are the Principalities, whose authority is the mailed fist of Necessary Evil, whose media mediate untruth, whose chief social method is betrayal and mass murder, whose religion is named Travesty, whose gods are Mars, Vulcan, Gog, and Magog.

An antiscripture blind to its own malignancy, helpless to grieve or renounce its crimes.

Which therefore can only repeat its crimes.

◆ ◆ ◆

The face is fused with the mask, to this point: that the mask becomes the only face of the "it" (the fallen ones, the given over, the "dwellers on earth," the not-yet human, the idol makers and shakers) — the only face of the great "it."

These to be named, unveiled, unmasked, be it noted, but never can this be done by themselves — a blind society, a giant named Polyphemus.

The giant is unmasked only by scripture, which knows both God and evil. Unmasked the likes of Ezekiel, who suffers at the hand of the giant — even as he offers the giant an only hope.

◆ ◆ ◆

The human body is political; it is one with the "body politic." Such is implied here, in the death of the spouse, in the response exacted of Ezekiel. And finally in the impact on the people of the woman's death and the behavior of Ezekiel.

◆ ◆ ◆

It is through the nearest and dearest of one's life, the beloved, that one gains understanding of public connection and responsibility. And the beloved, be it noted, is no less noble, no less grieved for, for being a "sign."

Indeed, the sign, rightly understood, expresses the highest nobility of the beloved.

Christ and ourselves: Christ as "sign" of our nobility and calling. Christ the beloved spouse, we the bride.

◆ ◆ ◆

It would seem to follow that a purely "private" love, friendship, marriage, is a supreme fiction. Love leads beyond the beloved.

Those who would have it otherwise are in conflict with biblical testimony.

To celebrate a wedding in time of war, for instance, is a plain act of resistance.

In "taking" one another, in acceptance and affection and mutuality, one stands with all his heart against the ferocious rejection and mass "disposal" of multitudes, signified and enacted by war.

◆ ◆ ◆

It is not easy being God's friend. We see Yahweh constantly "bearing down" on his chosen one. And we are stunned, awed.

An agonizing interplay it is, with dizzying rhythms of life and death striking close and hard.

The drama of Ezekiel and his family must be played out publicly, crisis upon crisis, to illuminate the drama of the community, whether under siege in Jerusalem or in exile.

◆ ◆ ◆

As for the role of "those in charge," the elders and priests, the meaning of this social drama is deliberately concealed.

Such is in the interest of the collaborators — an interest which, one judges, dovetails nicely with the interest of the tyrant at the gates.

Dark upon dark; these leaders too have a role, hardly different from the role of the oppressor. Covertly they keep the people distracted from, ignorant of, the truth of their plight.

◆ ◆ ◆

And above all, they suppress any surmise or suggestion of a way out. They keep dangerous memories suppressed, dangerous questions from being raised.

At all cost the power of memory must be weakened or obliterated. That power which relentlessly questions authority. Where did we come from, and why (Were we not once free?)? And why must we accept our enslavement (Why are we not now free?)?

And as to the future, another question, unmentionable, absolutely forbidden: Through whom, at whose behest and beckoning, shall we walk free? And when? A Moses in our midst?

◆ ◆ ◆

Nothing of this. Let it fall heavy upon the populace, a dead weight, a pure, unchangeable plight; no relief lies on the horizon, for none is possible.

◆ ◆ ◆

The exile, the horrid social dislocation, for many the end of the world. And the elders of Jerusalem, like a coven of quislings, settle in, continue to serve the tyrant well.

They are silent; all should be silent. They question nothing, no form of authority however inhuman or overweening.

Thus they serve to normalize the common plight, imbed it deep in "the nature of things."

In time, enslavement takes on an icy look of permanence, a metaphysical law. Thus it is decreed: some are enslaved; others are masters.

◆ ◆ ◆

And among the elders, the law is transmogrified into "the will of God." This will be harped on, in season and out. A double bind, human and divine, upon the dignity of all.

At this point, personal, not to say social, liberation becomes simply unimaginable. We are what we are what we are....

Others, inhuman though they be in ethos and behavior, have defined our humanity, thrusting the definition like the blade of a sword deep in our being.

To this we no longer object. We are simply weary and, at the same time, grateful for "being taken care of."

Thus the regression.

◆ ◆ ◆

Ezekiel and the elders.

He and they stand, as is evident, in a like predicament, the humiliation of exile.

Again and again Ezekiel is at pains to note the fact, the year, month, day, of this or that event, always relative to the duration of those terrible years.

◆ ◆ ◆

He is like a solitary prisoner marking on a blank wall the days of his bondage. Each night, crossing off a day. As though he whispered to his soul, "I may indeed be a prisoner, a slave, but I was not always such. Nor shall I always be such. There was a before; there will be an after."

◆ ◆ ◆

He knows his plight; he is unreconciled. He grinds his teeth in anger and frustration; he does harsh time; he detests the humiliation of his estate.

The days go by, somehow. "See, with a spot I damn..." He crosses them out one by one, each a dragon slain. The X is a sign, a reminder to his soul: Do not forget. Taste it and shudder, the bitter aloes of memory.

We shall be free.

This day of exile, awful as it is, constricting of soul and body, is not all of reality. Far from it.

This one knows something about "otherwise," "otherwhere," "otherwhen."

Memory is a nest of brooding alternatives; the egg of the future nears its term.

◆ ◆ ◆

He also has a map in mind: a homeland, a holy city where his heart dwells. No matter that it lies in ruins; we shall return and rebuild!

Thus the tyrant is defeated. The prisoner's memory has not been deadened, amortized, delivered over, bargained away.

◆ ◆ ◆

I remember the foul, noisy, pullulating camps where the Palestinian people are condemned, for generations now. Children, thousands of them, have been born in the camps, know no other setting. And yet the memories are passed on; the children can draw a detailed map — where their home stood, in such and such a village.

No matter that the home was bombed out of existence, on this or that occasion of "collective punishment," a brutal Nazi expedient.

No matter that, long since, the village has been seized and occupied by settlers.

The women remember; their clothing, its color, embroidery, style, is indigenous to that (lost) village. They sing the songs as well.

The past, alive, vibrant. Costly memory, not nostalgia. The past as guarantor of the future.

◆ ◆ ◆

Only imagine! Ezekiel remembers so vividly what once was (and surely shall be!) that on occasion he is literally carried away, transported back to Jerusalem, back, then forth again to Babylon. Time, an uneasy cradle of rebirth!

It is as though he were held close in a providential hand, neither totally here in exile, nor there in memory; the memory that is alive with prospect.

An image — a divided man, he of hither and yon, of time and eternity, of this world and another.

Thereby to be accounted and honored as fully human. And the honor accruing all the more; because his humanity flourishes against all odds.

◆ ◆ ◆

We ponder the duality of this great spirit; it is in fact a strength, a resource, a mysterious freedom. He sees the Jerusalem that was, intact and splendid. Then he sees the city fallen, the drovers, the exiles. And he knows the why of it all.

He sees more — possibility, a dawn, return, and restoration.

Like a full vessel, he contains the memory of the tribe. Even his existence, dire and deprived, his uneasy access to God — these are a form of hope, embodied and available.

What once was, shall again be. What we once were, we shall again be.

◆ ◆ ◆

It is against this stormy hope, unextinguished and so precarious, a flame in high wind, that one hears the thunders of his terrible diatribes — against idolatry above all.

Idolatry throttling hope. Idolatry a sluttish assimilation of very soul, a betrayal of the patrimony of the faith — and all for a mess of pottage. He has cried havoc upon it!

It is his vocation, his dignity — that cry.

◆ ◆ ◆

He remarks the dates with such exactness! Hope, bizarre and secret though it be, beats on. For sake of the exiles, for his own; hope against hope.

He counts the days, subversive stroke upon stroke. The days until — what?

Is he awaiting a Moses? Is he himself a Moses?

◆ ◆ ◆

The mood shifts are harsh, as a prisoner's are bound to be. Day by day, hour by hour, up and down the waves beat and beat.

Sense of dignity, worth, publicly sanctioned esteem — up goes his spirit as Yahweh intervenes, speaks on his behalf. Then down he plunges; the one of no account, a public fool in motley.

Depression to exaltation — to depression, like a vane in a gale.

◆ ◆ ◆

That foolish miming of God knows what. That bizarre behavior of his, unashamed and bold.

Come now, does he not himself undermine the claim to speak in God's name? Would a true prophet invite his own humiliation and downputting?

And all such besotted antics, as he insists obsessively, by very ordinance of God!

Thus the irony, violent and wrenching.

◆ ◆ ◆

Over against the prophet we have the elders. They are like birds of prey, clinging precariously to a cliff side. Even in exile, they hold fast; their pride of place reasonably intact; legislative, judicial, cultic.

Ostensibly they hold the tribe together, by rite and rote.

Can they not be relied on, these remnants of an ancient institution? Do they not stand up to the Babylonian tyrant, taking his lightning bolts to themselves, shielding the people from the worst?

Are they not the chosen mediators? Do they not embody an authority crucial to common survival?

In consequence do they not merit gratitude and respect, as they skillfully render the present crisis bearable, bespeaking (more, embodying) the lost greatness, linking the national downfall with yesterday's high noon?

Thus goes the conventional wisdom. These gray eminences are historically reassuring.

◆ ◆ ◆

It is of some interest to note that Ezekiel neither raises nor answers such questions as occur — occur perhaps at the eager instigation of the elders themselves!

But then again, we have noted that conventional wisdom is hardly his forte.

◆ ◆ ◆

Is there a dark side to this rosy picture?

Do the elders in fact urge on the people a subdued nostalgia for a remote "golden age," long gone?

Do they empty the veins of the venturesome and bold?

Does not their mix of religio-polity (better, their politics of "peace at a price, lest worse befall") offer a stark contrast to the outright resistance of an Ezekiel?

And is not the contrast a clue — to the disfavor they merit from Yahweh, the fury they occasion, as though indeed their will were worlds apart from the divine will?

◆ ◆ ◆

That resistance of Ezekiel. It takes the form of a goad, a reminder, a refusal to allow the exiles the sweet nostrum of forgetting.

Of forgetting cause and effect, sin and consequence.

No, Remember! is his cry. Remembering, you ensure a chastened return. Forgetting, you lose all.

◆ ◆ ◆

Exile, slavery, can become bearable, then desirable, a diet of sweet lotus.

Forgetting is the porcine outcome of the ancient myth. Humans are transformed to swine, dumb to their plight, turned earthward, numb likewise to yesterday and tomorrow.

◆ ◆ ◆

The elders, in sum, seem a rather safe, prosaic, even pedantic relic, a planet whose sun is setting.

Ezekiel has in their regard, questions, questions. Are these to be relied upon, to honor the public trust?

He notes (and would have us note) the doubts that arise. These eminences tread softly, urge by word and example that others walk straight and narrow, keep mum, salvage such vestiges of the past as may serve to make the present bearable.

◆ ◆ ◆

Ezekiel, literally one against many; almost one thinks, mad against sane.

Of a sudden, and as though out of nowhere, like a bolt of lightning — the challenge.

His warrant invites a close look.

You take him or leave, as temperament or mood of hope or despair impels.

Beyond doubt the argument he offers is circular; he is to be believed because he says he is to be believed. He has access to God because he says so. . . .

The claim, whatever its merit, has immediate repercussions.

◆ ◆ ◆

Two versions of life in the world (so awful a world, theirs!) emerge. Sides are drawn, a fierce conflict ensues. Ezekiel or the elders? The stuff of high drama, of tragedy even.

The prophet, it shortly becomes clear, is no mediocre dreamer, content to dwell in the shadow of event, easily put to silence.

He enters the public square and abruptly proposes a debate.

On the moment the agora becomes an arena, rife with argument and conflict.

He challenges fiercely the status quo commended by the elders, a social pattern they (embody and) commend. According to their ethos, it is carved and set in stone.

In sum: there shall be whips and tyrants and overseers. And there shall be victims and slaves. There shall be patient bent backs, brick ovens, straw or no straw, the cramped existence of those who are bought and sold in the bullish slave market of empire. Slaves, who count for nothing, whose hope is long extinguished.

This, the will of Yahweh.

◆ ◆ ◆

But the tongue of Ezekiel strikes like a lash against such religion — the sanctioning of an ugly status quo into dogmatic inevitability.

A religion of quislings.

◆ ◆ ◆

He tweaks their venerable beards, for a shameful delict against the common good; they have "normalized" the exile.

Fact and metaphor, the exile is crucial to understanding, to response and refusal; exile, the common plight.

All said, all suffered — rightly understood the bitter herb of exile must be accounted a salvation. Taste it, detest it, reject it. Let your guts revolt.

But the truth of the common situation has been robbed of its bitterness and sting.

◆ ◆ ◆

If exile becomes a norm, we are no longer in exile.

In such wise memory as a faculty of resistance, a summoning of truth, a beckoning to "come out, my people," is obliterated.

Settle down, settle in! You are now, and shall interminably be, a species of settlers.

Intermingle, intermarry, assimilate, as Yahweh quotes the elders: "We shall be like the nations, like the people of foreign lands, serving wood and stone" (20:32).

◆ ◆ ◆

This is the persuasion of these artful dodgers: to make the intolerable bearable, usual, normal, even welcome.

Are they so benign after all, these leaders? Or is their benignity a cover? For what? Betrayal?

One holds one's ears; an explosion is in the offing.

◆ ◆ ◆

Ezekiel "acts out" the hidden truth in all its bitterness and grandeur.

The people watch, wonder, mock — learn?

As to the possibility of learning, our account is hardly encouraging. Yahweh declares it unequivocally: the people will not learn; they will refuse the truth.

◆ ◆ ◆

Still, "Give them a chance!" we all but cry.

It is almost as though a prevailing pessimism on high were blocking the mind. Is Yahweh playing the bleak predestinationist?

How are a people to change their ways, if God declares them incapable of doing so?

(We have the like gloomy view of human capacity in Isaiah. And Jesus goes along, quoting Isaiah approvingly [Luke 8:10]. We are, it would seem, stuck where we stand.)

◆ ◆ ◆

Here contrary claims are laid out, mixed, even contrary messages. First, the way of the elders. And the swift intervention of Yahweh casts a merciless light on the quality of their faith.

They call it faith, knowing little of the genuine article.

Which is to say, they hold in mind a random collection of inert truths, concerning a God always "elsewhere." No living signs. Their God is nebulous and abstract, one whose presence (or absence, the two amount to much the same) creates a vast fogbound area of moral leeway.

Thus the elders, without visible remorse, steer their office in the direction of — betrayal. They become the lackeys of worldly masters.

◆ ◆ ◆

Their God cannot be imagined as raging, a Lear shouting aloud on behalf of the inarticulate, excluded, and victimized.

Their religion implies little or nothing of loss or suffering, requires little or nothing of accountability or consequence.

As the saying goes, they have "internalized" the exile, normalized its abhorrent abnormality.

And in virtue of their office, they urge a like attitude on others.

◆ ◆ ◆

Another process, roughly parallel to the first, also gets underway. Even as these leaders integrate the exile they externalize the faith. A matter of rote and rule, and no rocking the skiff.

◆ ◆ ◆

Worse, should such words as "Freedom now!" be launched on the air (or scrawled in a public place!), these exalted ones would join with the oppressors in denouncing the perpetrators.

Thus the elders serve as guardians of the vocabulary of enslavement, moral avoidance, ambiguity, duplicity, "doublespeak, don't think."

"Better a live jackass than a dead lion."

Orwellian. "Slavery is freedom!"

The implication being evident: know it, yield. Alternatives do not exist.

◆ ◆ ◆

Long before, such as these lost the reality of God as liberator.

Who, after all, in the palmy days of yore, when this claque prospered on their own ground and the temple was resonant with worship — who was in need of liberation?

They absorbed the deity into a status quo; secure, their interests were elegantly served.

◆ ◆ ◆

In plain truth, in those years they lost true God in false worship, and in trafficking with the nations.

It is hardly to be thought, then, that faith would be restored and held fast, in the hard circumstance of exile.

In both settings, truth told, assimilation to "the nations" occurred. First by way of power, then by way of powerlessness.

◆ ◆ ◆

The interests of the elders, their coherence with the tyrant, these remain carefully unstated, masked.

Thus the approach to Ezekiel.

What word from on high might be deemed "useful to our people"? Unstated: "useful as well to the designs of ourselves and our masters"?

DEATH AND THE BELOVED

To return to the death of the prophet's wife: Ezekiel breaks our hearts; how ardent, yielding, lucid is this mystic thrice exiled, this spirit of intractable courage.

"So I spoke to the people in the morning, and in the evening my wife died. And on the next morning, I did as I was commanded."

It is all quite laconic, the grief closely reined in.

◆ ◆ ◆

Death is the sign. Not the idea of death, or the prospect of death, not death as possible or probable.

The warning and warrant of God are served. In a drama of terror, death strikes home, close; exacted is the death of a beloved.

A terrifying pedagogy.

The instruction goes on, relentless: "Make no mourning for the dead."

◆ ◆ ◆

Death has invaded the house.

Is he then to go about, as though life were fairly equable, and he an unfeeling churl?

He is forbidden the rituals and rhythms that allow for grief and assuagement of grief.

◆ ◆ ◆

It is evening; the claim of death lies heavy on the house.

The people hear of his loss. They gather, view his comportment, and are astonished. His demeanor is composed, no sign or trace of tears.

Only the slightest of concession is allowed him; it stops the heart to think of it. He is permitted to "sigh, but not aloud."

◆ ◆ ◆

Why is a second burden laid on the first? What must it mean to lose the "delight of your eyes, the desire of your soul" — as though God knew well the love between these two, and the loss?

And then, to be denied all befitting ceremony of loss?

◆ ◆ ◆

I thought: the story implies a love that encircles three — Yahweh, the prophet, the unnamed spouse. A harsh and dreadful love.

And then a larger circle encompasses the smaller. The larger includes the community of exiles, their social affliction and loss of all, of land and home and temple.

The drama unfolds. It implies: the people too are teachable, suffering may yet issue in a lesson grasped.

◆ ◆ ◆

Loss to Ezekiel. And an equivalent loss shortly to be borne by the exiles.

Word of the catastrophe is neatly dovetailed into a sentence of compassion concerning the loss of "their stronghold, their joy and glory, the delight of their eyes and their heart's desire, their sons and daughters."

◆ ◆ ◆

Again our sense of time and place is shaken.

A fugitive arrives (where, when, to whom?) with the awful news: the holy city has fallen.

And Ezekiel's tongue is loosened.

◆ ◆ ◆

An interrupted life indeed.

We had a previous hint (3:22–27) that for a period of some three years, during the final siege of Jerusalem, this voluble man was stricken mute. Gesture and mime must replace speech. For events had moved terribly beyond words.

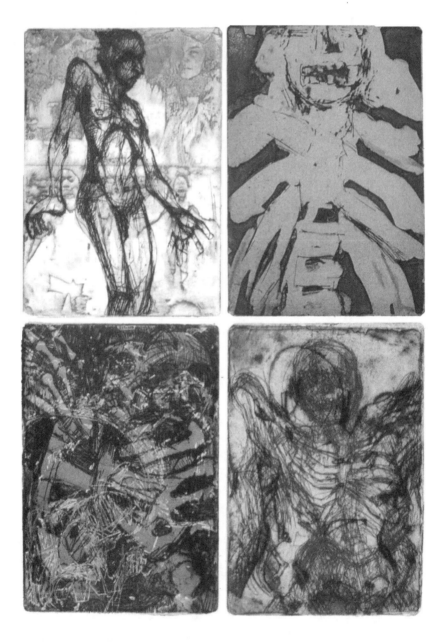

(Has something of the like occurred to us also — situations, events, losses that lie somewhere in a no-word land, in a kind of rain forest of tears? If so, we are in good company.)

◆ ◆ ◆

Psychologizing has its limits, as the Bible implicitly warns.

Again and again, the silence of great spirits is commended to us — a silence that is itself a sign of the limits of speech.

We summon the silence of Christ before Pilate, implying scorn, reproof, and rebuke in the face of illegitimate authority.

We recall his love of silence and solitude, his mysterious communing with the Father. We think of the silence that lies between his words, images, episodes. Between one footfall and the next. Between heartbeats.

We follow him, we ask whither is he bound, and why, on what errand of mercy, inclusion, compassion? He answers not a word.

◆ ◆ ◆

Time, we are reminded — we need time to remember and ponder. Give us time. And above all, give us a capacity for listening.

Denying ourselves speech, undergoing the discipline of silence, we too, like the exiles, may become teachable.

◆ ◆ ◆

Yet in the plight of Ezekiel, more is implied than silence.

He is struck mute. The power of formulating rational speech is denied him.

For three years he endures the affliction.

What brought it about? Was it his knowledge of a vast social cataclysm in the offing?

Whatever the cause, the knowledge is his alone.

Secret, it is a prospect, one thinks, apt to strike one dumb. In a sense a prospect worse than the event.

YAHWEH, ANTIIMPERIALIST
Ezekiel 25, 26, 27, 35

As to the purport of the tirades that follow, let us surmise. Ammon, Edom, Moab, Philistia, Tyre, each lies under the whiplash of rhetoric.

This or that empire falls; a second great entity governed by opposing ideology takes to rejoicing.

This is the story of the conflicting empires. Each speaks endlessly of the advantage of its system over the other, whether in economics, military might, political systems, freedoms enjoyed by its citizens, and so on.

The reality is other than the message.

◆ ◆ ◆

Nearer the truth, each empire is an image of the other. Each fits to a nicety the image held by the other.

Each reigns supreme in its orbit of influence on the world stage; each is riddled through and through with friction, distrust, envy. Each rattles its armaments, threat, and counterthreat.

Each is feverish with violence and rapacity.

A spectator foreign to either might have thought (or God might have thought), as the superpowers warily circle each other, each guarding its "sphere of influence" — might have thought: the world is too small, too vulnerable, to survive such monstrosities.

And now one is victor, the other fallen.

◆ ◆ ◆

"Mortal one, this is my message to the victor.
You are not the victor. Your day is coming as well.
My Day.
As your enemy fell, so shall you fall. Tell them.

"How you once gloried, how you too shall fall!
Did you not understand, you also, that for all your devious diplomacy, for all your weaponry, the fate of your rival is to be yours also?

Because of incursions and rapacity, because murder is your skill and obsession — consequence will pursue you like a coven of furies.

You have loosed a torrent of blood; the blood cries out from the ground.

The sword you wielded will turn against you.

You said in your pride: this or that nation is delivered up to us; we have prevailed.

I hear your boast — no ill shall strike, no consequence or judgment be placed against our actions.

The boast is vain.

As you have done to others, be it done to you.

"In the Gulf slaughter, your armaments fused the sands of the desert to a sea of glass.

Your warriors returned home to a delirium of folly, flags, a wicked joy.

But the winds veer about, a desert storm blows in your direction.

Your behavior will not long prevail. I swear it by my holy name.

"Bloodshed and idols!

Your works are already judged. Exile, famine, the sword be your lot.

On that day, which is My Day, a palsy will seize the limbs of your great ones.

The downfall of the proud, be it tardy or precipitous, is inevitable!" (25ff.)

◆ ◆ ◆

The principalities! They lay claim to the world. Alert and vigorous, they are embodied again and again in this or that superpower.

Strange though: these empires, proud and splendid, coruscating with riches — they come to the same end.

He keeps harping on the theme, this most intransigent, dire-tongued, unassimilable Ezekiel!

Beware! is his word. He utters it with fierce passion, as the very word of God. You high and mighty ones, you then would play God?

You are mere mortals, vulnerable as the beggar at your gate.

◆ ◆ ◆

If God exists, the God of Ezekiel, judgment follows crime.

An indictment against the nations must be drawn up.

This challenging of the ways of the world is an old biblical story. (A story despised and ignored, one must add, by those against whom it is spoken.)

◆ ◆ ◆

Has God not spoken in this wise before, telling of awful eventualities, and the worsening, by reason of blindness, of the spiritual estate of the powerful?

◆ ◆ ◆

To speak of our own country: American leaders in the twentieth century have devised policies that for their malevolence and finesse and skills of mass murder, beggar the imagination.

To speak only of Salvador: for a decade of war multitudes perished; innocents, peasants, highly placed clerics, labor leaders, catechists, the lowly and nameless.

Finally, tardily, in 1993 the truth is revealed, in one document after another. The Americans, through the CIA, the School of the Americas, limitless military funding in favor of the juntas, are complicit in the slaughter.

But the reports shake only minor thrones, those of the client killers, the hired guns. It is shortly made clear that the major perpetrators, their decisions cannily hidden, will tolerate no word of accountability.

The worst among them in any case have fled the political scene. Debts were paid, silence bought.

And what good is served (so the argument goes) by exhuming the past? It had best lie buried, a corpse, or a multitude of corpses. Dust to dust.

◆ ◆ ◆

No.

Accountability, reality, judgment! There are truths that must be spoken, recorded, inscribed in the recusant human heart.

Granted the truths go against the grain, are unpalatable or untimely.

No matter. They convey the hope of generations, an only hope, an anthropology of hope. They denote a persistent tradition of the human.

They trace in the filth of time's track, a dividing line.

The line is faint, all but obliterated. Nevertheless it can be discerned. The finger of God has traced it; here the noble and human, there the vile and deviant.

ONCE MORE, THE FALL FROM GRACE
Ezekiel 28

We are to conjure a splendid empire, favored by God and nature and the luck of the strong. Our own, America.

Sea, land, prairie, mountain, desert, all in consonance and contrast, seasonally beautiful and bracing.

Armies, weapons, bombers, fleets scour the earth, athwart upstart or trespasser.

Do rivals threaten? It is all in vain.

Colonies and their client rulers bow obeisant, faithful to the polity of empire.

Manifest your destiny.

◆ ◆ ◆

Your business in the world is — business.

Billions of *dollare,* riches beyond computing.

A superscription etched on your coinage: IN GOD WE TRUST!

And universal dominion and high culture (and religion?) on beck and call. Indeed the scope of your economy is clear in the international entrepreneurs who trade and prosper...

◆ ◆ ◆

...and who in a moment lost everything: "gold, silver, precious stones and pearls; goods of linen, purple cloth, silk, and scarlet cloth; all kinds of rare woods, objects made of ivory,...of bronze, iron, and marble; and cinnamon, spice, incense, myrrh, and frankincense; wine and oil, flour and wheat, cattle and sheep, horses and carriages...." And then the moral nadir: the empire trades in "bodies, and the souls of people" (Rev. 18:11ff.; the Good News Bible has "slaves, and even human lives," which seems inadequate to the Greek *pseukay* and *soma;* the RSV has "slaves, that is, human souls").

In any case, the point seems clear: the empire holds in possession, and trades in, both bodies and souls.

◆ ◆ ◆

Not idly, one thinks, does the author of Revelation place this awful truth, this enslavement and cannibalistic economy, last on the list of imperial commodities.

As a warning, an invitation to pondering?

What claims of patriotism, consumerism, religious observance even, lie heavy upon us, unexamined, backbreaking, soul-diminishing.

◆ ◆ ◆

And the aptest description of imperial splendor is offered, ironically enough, by an angel.

At once destroyer and mourner, the supernal being views the collapsed empire: "the music of harps and of human voices, of players of the flute and trumpet, never to be heard in you again! No workman in any trade to be found in you again; the sound of the millstone heard no more! Never again will the light of a lamp be seen in you; no more will the voices of brides and grooms be heard in you" (Rev. 18:21–23).

Then judgment is rendered against the cultural matrix — economic piracy and state-sponsored religion: "Your merchants were the most powerful in the world, and with your sorcery you deceived all peoples."

◆ ◆ ◆

Likewise Tyre and Sidon and every empire since.

The beginnings were innocent enough: blameless you were in your conduct, from the day you were created.

Shortly, alas, imperial appetites arose, the innocence evaporated in greed:

Evil was found in you, the result of your far flung trade, your business.... You did such evil in buying and selling that your very sanctuaries were corrupted. (Ezek. 28:15, 16, 18)

Behold the economics of Ezekiel — and by strong implication, of Ezekiel's God.

Matters, one thinks, were not so baldly stated before; the connection between money, violence, and certain forms of religion.

◆ ◆ ◆

And yet, and yet, always and everywhere, the gods are denied the last word.

They are toppled, scattered. The promise holds: Yahweh will manifest his holiness; the remnant will be gathered once more, in a land restored.

And this too signifies.

The epiphany granted Ezekiel offers no vague theism, but a concrete hope.

◆ ◆ ◆

The promise is gentle and pastoral. The remnant have sojourned afar, exiles, victims of empire. They have suffered heavily and long. Now at long last, light has dawned.

They are bound homeward, to claim the land for their own, to build homes and plant vines. Through a tardy fidelity, they have wrung victory from disaster (28:25, 26).

THE PHARAOH AND FRIENDS, DEFLATED
Ezekiel 29, 30, 32

First, the immortal one of Egypt.

Yahweh speaks:

"Behold the pharaoh, what I make of him —
a monstrous crocodile!

He crawls about on his belly, lumbers hither and yon, snorting, splenetic.

The land is his domain, and the entire Nile as well. Or so he claims.

Daily he scouts the land for prey. Sated, like an unwieldy log, he rolls into the water.

Huge as an ambulatory mountain, he displaces the waters of the great river.

A tidal wave at his coming! Filth, silt, turbulence in his wake!

Headwater to estuary, he lunges and roams, a ponderous satrap.

The Nile is his element, he trumpets.

Even — his own creation!

Folly could devise no greater absurdity.

"The appetite and ire of the king of crocodiles!
A monstrosity. What then to be done!
I, Yahweh, will tell you.
Pharaoh-crocodile, I am the fisher of such as you.
Tackle, rod, net, hook, I lie in wait.
My bait is irresistible.
I offer fat worms, newts, clams, frogs, snails, a menu of crawling subterranean creatures.
Dredged and forked and raked from the river bed, they mime the fate of—yourself, the pharaoh.

"Hook, line, sinker! I play the line, the bait dangles before his eyes.
His jaws close with a great snap!
Now I have you, monster.
By main force I hold you, twitching and raging in midair.

"Watch. In a dizzying arc, I fling you far and wide, to the four winds.
No more Nile to harbor and nourish, upbear and conceal, no inundation teeming with your prey!
Enough of you, and more. Enough preying and stalking and shattering the peace of creation with your bellowing.
You sprawl there in the desert, jaws working in spasm, starved and helpless, a giant undone.
Die then.
Feed others with your flesh, you cannibal.

"I summon to a banquet the creatures you terrified, brawling and stalking about.
Birds of air and beasts of land, eat and be filled and fear not!
The great mail-jacketed ruffian is brought low.

"When you have rotted and dried under the desert sun, pharaoh, I cut you in pieces, hide and teeth and claws.
Crocodile king, I dispatch those relics of yours to the kings of earth: to the ape king, the cat king, the gorgon king, the griffin king.
Behold my gift, and tremble!
They blanch and cry out in fear, their knees turn to water.
An eye looks up at them, an eye plucked from the skull, filmy, rancorous, dead. Or a scaly limb. Or a jagged edge of teeth and jaw.

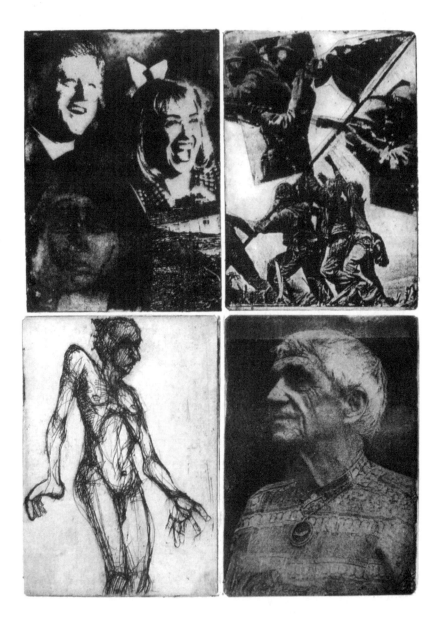

To each according to need!

"The kings behold with horror the desiccated relics — a bone, a snatch of hair, the torn hide of the king of the beasts.

How the mighty are fallen! they cry.

The pharaoh who ranged far and wide, over water and land, north, south, vast as the meandering imperium of the Nile, the king at whose thunders the very earth shuddered with fear — the king of the crocodiles is dead!

Yahweh: that day, at length My Day.

"Tell it, mortal one.

They are all vanished into the world of the dead.

In the First World War, by the millions; at Verdun, the Somme. And their poets, innocents all: Benn, Sassoon, Trakl, Owen, perished.

And the Russians, long-suffering under the lash of Hitler, then of Stalin. Stalingrad: twenty million dead. The poets and mystics too: Akhmatova, Pasternak, Mandelstam, Mayakovski, Tsvetayeva. All, all gone.

Pronounce these names, mortal one: Hiroshima, Nagasaki, Dresden, Coventry." (29ff.)

♦ ♦ ♦

A most democratic being, this god of technique. His decree: children die, the aged too. No distinction, no exception. All disappeared, away and away.

The poets are quenched: Brecht, Prevert, Quasimodo, Char, Oppen, Swir, Thomas, Lowell, Grass.

Those innocents, singers, mourners, vanished, down and down to the world of the dead.

Indeed that world beyond the Styx is long since overcrowded.

And the boats arrive on the hour, their spaces teeming with ghosts.

♦ ♦ ♦

Old Charon's mood is foul. He thwacks with a lusty oar the multitude who clamber aboard, endangering the passage.

And the voices, a pentecost of tongues ablaze! Eyes blank with shock, dull with incomprehension.

Vietnamese, Cambodians, Laotians in vast numbers, then Grenadians, Panamanians, Salvadorans, Nicaraguans, the indigenous peoples of Guatemala, multitudes of Iraqis.

♦ ♦ ♦

Here, among the dead, celebrate an advantage of note over the world of the living. These spirits are entirely freed from mortal needs, food or shelter.

They are mere shades of shades, marmoreally calm and peaceable. Were they great warriors on earth? Here, if anger sparks, if they reach for a sword as of yore — see, they brandish broken reeds, woven straws.

Still, old ways die hard. The pretense, the empty strut of glory! They drift about in accouterments of war: uniforms, medals, epaulets.

All a vain show! Ghosts on parade, utterly innocuous (Ezek. 31: 14–18).

DOWN, DOWN TO THE NETHERWORLD, THE GREAT TREE OF CREATION
Ezekiel 31

"Mortal one, hear.

Another image of the pharaoh.

Flourishing mightily, he is like the central tree of the garden of creation.

How describe the beauty, the resilience and strength of this noble being?

Behold him, a very pillar and pivot of creation.

Humans pause, stock still in awe, take direction, north or south, from him. Shade and refreshment from him.

And if one should gaze on high — it was as though the thrust of his limbs upheld the very heavens.

"Shall I name him 'tree of the knowledge of good and evil'?
Stature, awesome presence!

Hear it, the boast, a tremor of pride in the high branches: None like unto me!

"Thus from the beginning, the mighty one nurtured seeds of greatness — and seeds of destruction.

Sufficient unto himself, for generations he flourished and withstood.

No wind served to topple him. Or so it seemed.

Winds blew: now lightly, now with fierce vigor.

A great storm arose; like a gigantic hand, it seized on the tree, shook it to root.

Ever so slightly the tree swayed.

Then it grew agitated, shook as though in agony, a very Lear of the forest.

A crack of doom! See, all about, fauna less firmly rooted, tumble to ground!

The furious winds grew still. One tree stood.

Its splendor unmarred, unbroken.

In those days, giants dwelt upon the earth!

"But wait.

One day the forest is loud with unwonted bustle and skirmish.

There arrives a troop of woodsmen, armed with cutters, saws, axes.

They surround the king of the forest.

"This immemorial, lofty being! They care not a whit.

Five royal centuries it gazed on high, heaven and earth captive to a net of glory —

all, alas, to be undone in an hour.

"They set to work, these unconscious brawns.

The imperial one, hacked, wounded grievously —

then — 'Down!'

It falls and pauses and falls, slow, slow, grandly curving like a sea wave, a wall of China, a rampart.

The reverberations of that fall — they sound and resound.

Earth itself is wounded; a vast groan arises from the soul of creation.

From the ruin a column of sawdust arises like a ghost, dissolves in the choked air.

Sunshot day or befogged, summer or winter, what difference! Seasons, times, perdurances, dignities, fealties, still center and noble outreach — all null and void.

The base is splayed out level with earth, a wooden star, convolveses for points.

A death sweat gathers in the rings of life." (31:2–14)

◆ ◆ ◆

Tears of a messiah! — pathetic fallacy for times grown tragic, gone awry.

◆ ◆ ◆

Dip hands in the essence!
It flows three or four weeks,
the season when in the south,
mocking birds,
sleepless with ecstasy,
raving, raise their cry —
O may all creatures live!

As though from the cave of creation,
whence the heartbeat of all things takes start,
a drumbeat slow and slower:
lamentation, the prelude,
the precise reconnaissance of death.

A final heartbeat. Then silence.
The stupendous one is fallen.

Feckless, the woodsmen trample about,
whistling a tune,
hacking at limbs and branches.
Job done. What care they? (31:15–18)

THE PROPHET AS SENTINEL
Ezekiel 33

"Mortal one, hear.
As a sentinel is appointed to walk the ramparts, lest an enemy
approach by stealth and overwhelm the city — so I appoint you.
Eye to the horizon, ear to the four winds, sound the alarm!
Note well my will, the terms of age-old covenant.
Keep watch then! This is a perverted people —
even the just among them try me sorely.

"And the evil ones try me more sorely yet.
Hair-splitting sophists all, they argue and speculate.
Thus: What if one were to turn from evil, render just weights
and measures, restore what was larcenously taken, what then?
Tell them (they already know it, these prestidigitators of the
spirit) this: past wickedness is canceled; judgment falls according
to present behavior.

"Yet I hear them sibilant murmur (this people once known as
my people): God is unjust!

I am cornered. I am hostage to mine own justice.

Tell them: I see you plain. I weigh you in the scales of each day's behavior."

It was the twelfth year, the tenth month, and the fifth day of our captivity.

I have told it before: how for a long time the hand of the Lord lay across my mouth, forbidding all speech.

I have told it: there arrived a survivor from the holy city. Jerusalem had fallen.

On the moment
Alleluia! the Lord
removed his hand.
Like a harp
in a burst of wind
after long becalming
sweetly, strongly attuned
I spoke once more!

And a mood devoid of comfort —

Yahweh: "They sit in the ruins of Jerusalem, a conventicle of fools. This their mad theme:

Our father Abraham seized this land for his own.

And look, we are a multitude. Shall the land not be irretrievably our own!

"Answer them: obsessed as you are with blood — bloody meats, bloodletting, offerings to bloody idols — shall the land be yours!

Abominable. You live by the sword, you die in your blood — and the land shall be yours!

Tell them. Death be your portion. Death by the sword, death by wild beasts, death by plague.

I shall make of city and countryside, far as the eye ranges, an indistinguishable wilderness. In the streets not a soul. On the mountains not a footfall.

They shall know at long last, that I am God.

"Mortal one, the time of exile hangs heavy.

In idleness the people while the hours away, squatting along the walls or in the doorways.

Lacking other diversion, someone idly proposes: Come, let us seek out the prophet. Who can tell, he may utter some word or other from Yahweh!

Willy-nilly, a crowd gathers.

Belief, hope, obedience? not a whit.

Lies pass from idle tongues to idle ears, greed and guile and wily words fester.

"And you, Ezekiel —

To this people no more than a wandering minstrel, ready with lightsome tunes.

Will you hum a tune, amuse them? — it ends, they scatter like a chaff.

No tunes for them; but dissonant, off-key, off-putting — the truth.

Speak. They will know (and all too late!) — a prophet has stood in their midst." (33:1ff.)

WOE TO THE FALSE SHEPHERDS!
Ezekiel 34

"Mortal one,
denounce the leaders of my people.
These have become the misleaders.
Stones for hearts, grasping hands!
Busy as hive-bound bees,
their honey store private, posted.

"Say to them: how you ensure
gross corporal well-being —
laden tables,
gleaming accouterments,
well-bred servants in shadow —
hinting
boundless resource, reserve.

" 'The hungry sheep look for us and are
not fed.'
I answer for them.
Shepherds witless as sheep —
Fools!
I am judgment.

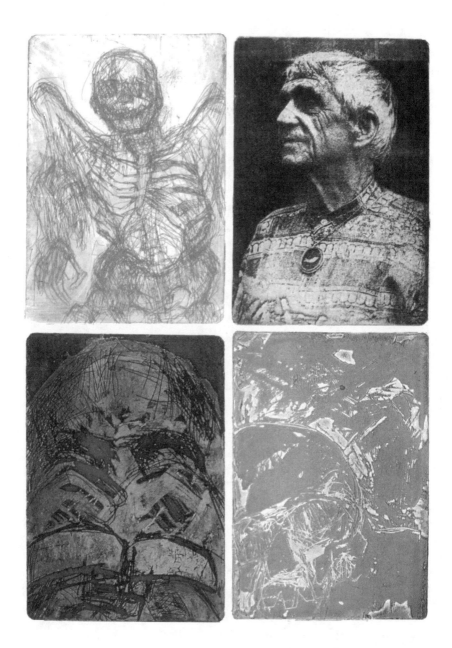

I am Lazarus at the gate —
        disregarded,
detritus, dust
of your rake's progress.

            "Prosecutor, jury, judge,
I pronounce, denounce;
            word of Yahweh!

        "I tip your table like a matchwood,
            and you, midcourse in orgy,
                stuporous,
            I bring low —
your great ones I drag
like offal to the gates,
hunger and rags your lot,
scabious sores, red
as verdict's capital,
        raw, uncial, summary —
                'Guilty!'

"Your crimes: gross negligence,
dereliction of duty, fraud,
heaping of benefits unearned,
despoiling of creation.

"Your charge, my flock —
    behold them
    neglected, distraught,
    wounded, afar wandering, prey
of ravening beasts —
for them I weep, them gather,
succor.

"Dear ones, but wait, patience!
Days of exile, famine, wild beasts —
            all ended!
        Brother sun, sister rain,
            kindly as I,
shine bright, fall gentle,
befriend, bring smiles to faces.

"No matter rumors,
    incantations, 'God

of power and might' —
　　not a whit availing.

"Would you seek me!
An old shepherd
ambles past your doorway,
　　his greyphized dog
nudging the sheep along.

"A shepherd, a clue —
long silences, eyes
roaming the flock ceaselessly,
　　counting, accounting —
and a crook's outreach
follows his glance,
keeping a witless lamb in line —
clues.

"Have done with this god,
　　this 'power and might'!
It sickens me —
malfeasance and muscle,
a godling Caesar,
seizing if he could, high heaven
(overbearing heaven,
high in your chancels).

"Ezekiel —
an old shepherd
would speak with you." (34:1ff.)

THE LAND, THE PEOPLE REBORN
Ezekiel 36

"Justice!
I, Yahweh, cry out for it.
No response.
You, bent on your own will.
The land stinks like an abattoir;
idols, blood rites!
An Ecclesiastes I sigh;
the sun brightens and fails,
and the days and nights;

and what is new under the sun?
I keep watch, I observe
this misbegotten race of mortals,
their foibles and follies —
it comes to this:
I, Yahweh, hereby resign.

"King, potentate, judge, overseer, primum mobile, pure existence, motor mundi —

Hereby all is deeded over. Take it for your own.

All and sundry, titles, honors, emoluments, inheritance, legacies, perquisites — hereby I hand over.

I will vanish into the hills and valleys, a shepherd, a dresser of trees, tradesman, farmhand, minstrel, storyteller, wandering fool.

My song I sing to the hills and trees; mayhap they will dance to my tune.

"Give ear then, forests, hills, valleys.

Who knows, all may not be lost.

Anonymous, dishonored, it may be I shall yet prevail.

Hills, valleys, gorges, streams, I breathe upon you, in you I live. In a good season you shall once again be seeded and planted and grow fecund.

"How love overmasters me!
Heart of my heart, my people,
this song for your sake —
sing the beauty of this land!
sing vine-keeper,
tree dresser, shepherd,
minstrel,
storyteller —
all for your sake!

"In my arms, you.
You, no longer
devouring, destroying.
You, never again
a Herod in the world!
No crime, no idols!

"I pluck from breast
your heart of stone,

your tocsin of violence,
muffled, funerary, implacable.

"I place in your breast
a heart of flesh,
breathe on you
new spirit,
and lo!
the world is made new —
fields lacy with grain,
trees groaning with fruits,
clouds raining
a gentle beneficence!

"The searing, forsaken desert —
end to end, an Eden!

"To work, my people!
From the ruins,
stone upon stone rises
new Jerusalem,
rosy as dawn!" (36:1ff.)

DRY BONES, TWO STICKS
Ezekiel 37

DRY BONES, DRY BONES

Yahweh:
"You, Ezekiel,
on you, my spirit!

"Like a driven cloud
ride aloft, range the earth.
Thunder from the cloud! a summons!
Come where dry bones lie,
a forest gone to stone,
a harvest of wrecked humans.

"Woe upon woe!
skulls of women
slender bones of children
bones wanton broken
skinny thigh bones of the aged

bones of the innocent
bones of executioners
torturers, the tortured
the gainly, the grotesque
snatched in the night,
starved in desert torment.

"The killing fields!
Bosnia, South Africa,
Iraq, Ireland,
Salvador (weep for Salvador!).

"Vast acreage of death,
once fields of birth —
fields of unutterable
scything and harvest!

(And in a moment, in a dark corner,
minds ruled by darkness,
thwarted, snuffed —
aborted, derided, put to naught!)

"(The courts and keeps,
the bridges of sighs,
the befouling works and pomps,
the empty grandeur, shameful acts
frozen in public monuments.
Armies like locust plagues,
generals preening, bombers scouring the skies.
I tot up the wars, the incursions,
the to-fro shock and echo of berserkers.
Have I populated the earth with monsters!)

        "Of the symphonic
        sweep and scope
        of my creation
        (which I in a mood of love
        dreamed into being),
        they make this —
        a petrified forest of death.

        "Bones, bones. Dry bones.
        But not forever, I swear it!

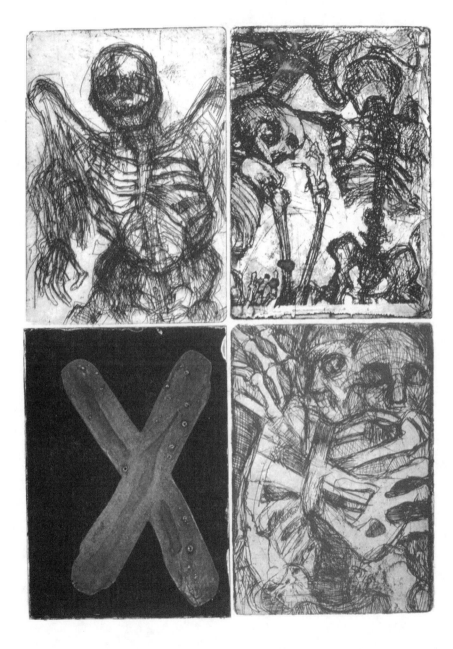

"Ezekiel,
stand in the killing fields.
Shall these bones live?
I said:
    Speak then to the bones.
    Say to them: Dry bones,
        hear the word of God —
            I
breathe my spirit upon you,
  you shall live!

"I weave your nerves anew,
I build flesh,
I stretch a living tegument;
    I breathe
sweetly, strongly —
  you shall live."

Ezekiel:
    I commanded.

And a rustling sound
as of leaves in autumn wind
  started
amid the dry bones.
A whisper, then a drumbeat!

    They stood erect, those bones,
and knitted firm!
skull to spine,
    hip bone to thigh bone,
        foot bone to ankle bone.

That Weaver of humans!
The bones together flew
cunning nerves and tendons,
flesh made fresh,
tender as the newborn.
Stock-still they stood,
like standing stones
spiritless
mere mime of the living.

Said to me:
"Summon the spirit, Ezekiel.

Come from the errant winds, my spirit.
Breathe on these bones, they shall live."

I spoke,
and the spirit entered the bones.
First a whisper,
then a drumbeat,
then reverberant —
a heartbeat!

They took breath once more! and
walked about! and
conversed one with another!
joyful, harmonious,
an immense throng, the newborn, the living!

Said to me:
"Behold the dry bones, how they live!
(Yet once on a time
these [and their keepers and killers,
echoed the words]
said in their hearts:
our plight is hopeless,
Death, come quickly.)

"Speak to them.
Say:
Death no dominion!
from graves, mausoleums, hecatombs —
Lazarine multitudes, come forth!

"Rejoice!
far from servitude!
enter the gates
of new Jerusalem!" (37:1–4)

◆ ◆ ◆

Thus the most famous passage in Ezekiel, one of the great extended
metaphors of all literature.

Elsewhere in the oracles, we are given a dozen or more of precise
dates, taking note of events, from the quotidian to the ecstatic —

here only   no date is noted
the   drawing   forth an event   placed
outside time's
(   )

◆ ◆ ◆

But the stupendous act is hardly outside place.

It occurs in a "valley of the last stand." There, Judea's last king clashed with the Babylonians.

It is specific bones, the bones of the violent, the bones of warriors that "shall live."

They too are victims, who have created victims.

◆ ◆ ◆

Thus the resurrecting Yahweh keeps pace, even with us, only slightly ahead of our clouded understanding.

Dazzling, bestirring us with contradictions, denunciations, rebukes, epiphanies of an absolute otherness.

Something other now.

Here we are advised implicitly: "Let the fallen warriors stand for all of you — who believe in warriors and war, whose hearts stand with them. I will raise even you, who have made of creation a wasteland, and called it Peace. Who have slain and been slain."

◆ ◆ ◆

On the face of the imagery
one is bound to conclude —
the act of God starts,
the arm is raised
at point of absolute zero: dry bones.
It is like the first breath of the spirit
the first day
of the first week of creation;
out of the void,
the genesis of all.

◆ ◆ ◆

And one misses perhaps, a further irony: it is Ezekiel, the rejected despised one, who stands at the center of the event, who is himself raised, the organ of the spirit. Ezekiel is summoned — to summon the dead.

He has been there; he knows the way back.

He stands there, viewing the petrified fallen forest of bones. He knows the scene; it has been his native landscape, for years and years.

Then, something untoward, unmerited (and yet merited), beyond imagining (but yes, within the vast purview of his imagining).

"[Yahweh said to me]: Speak to the bones. Say to them: Dry bones, hear the word of God."

We take note of the choice, and we take heart.

Behold the "mortal one." It is a zero, a despised outcast, the one who lurks at the edge of history, not once a protagonist, counting for little or nothing, standing desolate outside the mainstream of event and meaning, given over to "irrelevant" matters like sin and consequence and personal responsibility, this one who finds his situation beyond words, and confects mime of futile greatness and catastrophic outcomes. This is the chosen, this rejected one of the "chosen."

◆ ◆ ◆

An equivalent occurs: our prisoners of conscience.

One group, naming themselves audaciously the "Good News Plowshares," abode for months in a hideous warehouse in Newport News, subject to the constant clamor of TV, isolated from family and friends, awaiting trial and undoubted conviction and harsh extended jail time.

Another group, in December '93, entered an air force base in North Carolina and wrought brief symbolic damage, pouring their blood on a bomber deployed in the air war against Baghdad.

The group called itself the "Pax Christi and Spirit of Life Plowshares."

They too abode in the clutches of metronomic "justice," were jailed, tried, convicted, savagely sentenced.

◆ ◆ ◆

And Fr. Karl Kabat: five years for a nonviolent symbolic assault on a nuclear installation. With supreme grace and good will he takes the blow.

No reassuring public interest rests on these or their (our) cause; no media interest; no impact, as far as may be known, on weapons makers, buyers, sellers; no interruption of the secret throb and beat of this or that war in the making.

◆ ◆ ◆

One does what one must. That is all, or very nearly all. In so acting against the crude grain of the times, in the collective view (the church view as well), our prisoners are reduced to the equivalent of — a heap of their own bones.

The view is current also among a certain number of friends, who, faced with such an event, are rather quickly transformed into former friends.

From friends to the dry bones of friendship?

◆ ◆ ◆

Nothing could be imagined, it would seem, more useless, pitiful, "former," done with, dead, than the heap of desert bones Ezekiel is led to view — and to act upon.

◆ ◆ ◆

Once on a time they were alive, appallingly so. They were bloodily engaged in and swiftly cut down, in a "righteous cause."

Like every other conflict in history — righteous.

A special, almost antic irony rules the scene.

Who is this Yahweh, who here makes sport of us (of all of us)? Peacemakers take warning: it is the warriors, those honorable disciplined "just ones" of whatever "fatherland," Hector and Achilles and their like, who first of all (ahead of your virtuous selves, ahead of martyrs and saints and patriarchs and prophets) — feel their bones shake and rise and stand vertical under the thunders of the spirit. These it is who are summarily bidden forth from death.

◆ ◆ ◆

And then ourselves, and our prisoners. Who must be patient and endure and hope against hope, waiting upon an act of God. The second harvest, the late one.

◆ ◆ ◆

We once formed a community, or so we thought.

Fond our thought, as public events worsened, and the insatiable armaments and warriors and war-makers, like a species of carnivores, consumed the earth.

◆ ◆ ◆

Something became painfully apparent — invariably after the fact, after this or that "crime" of the Plowshares groups.

At a certain point it became clear that all along we had been a community — to a degree only.

Agreed, the circle of friends seemed in agreement; yes, our numbers prospered in a modest way.

Then, the crime; and friends walked away.

◆ ◆ ◆

Too bad, it was implied, that the group of resisters had acted so — irresponsibly. Matters had been going so well.

We were plugging along with this or that project, certainly useful, undeniably difficult. In the eyes of many, we and our work were admired, even emulated. We were serving the poor, the street people, housing and feeding the needy, succoring the dying.

And you Greg, and you Michele, greatly given to such good work.

And newly married! And shortly thereafter, separately jailed. Thereby violating, at one stroke, a number of conventional canons.

Such as the Plowshares people, it was alleged, had spoiled everything, had left a dark trail of discomfiture and confusion in their wake.

The moral of this: some bones remain quite lively, thumping away; bones of contention.

◆ ◆ ◆

But as to those dead bones, we have other echoes, other images:

This motif — the sufficiency of the infinitesimal — pervades Jesus' teaching. One does not need great faith, he says, but only as much as a mustard seed — which is to say, an almost imperceptible amount. . . .

Take the mustard seed, the tiniest seed this carpenter had ever seen. To those looking for a mighty nation like the towering cedar promised in Ezekiel 17, Jesus mockingly offers a prodigious — shrub! (Walter Wink, "The Power of the Small")

◆ ◆ ◆

The episode is a vivid illustration of, among other things, the death, and then the resurrection, of hope:

We should all feel near to despair in some sense, because this semi-despair is the normal form taken by hope in a time like ours. Hope without any sensible or tangible evidence on which to rest. Hope in spite of the sickness that fills us. Hope married to a firm refusal to accept any palliatives or anything that cheats hope by pretending to relieve apparent despair.

And I would add that for you especially hope must mean acceptance of limitations and imperfections and the deceitfulness of a nature that has been wounded and cheated of love and of security; this too we all feel and suffer. Thus we cannot enjoy the luxury of a hope based on our own integrity, our own honesty, our own purity of heart. (Thomas Merton, letter to Czeslaw Milosz)

◆ ◆ ◆

The setting is Babylon. The exiles are uprooted from homeland, family, temple. And once set down in place, they are increasingly demoralized.

It is as though Yahweh were plunging them in utter darkness; Ezekiel's uncompromising judgments, purportedly arriving direct from God, all but break the heart.

The sins, the crimes, the defaults! At every level of life and authority, memory is stirred up by the prophet.

It is as though the prophet were mordantly stoking a fire under a witch's brew, stirring and stirring the volatile juices of memory. An unsavory stew he holds to their lips! The people must drink to the lees, must remember and mourn and reconcile.

◆ ◆ ◆

He mimes and mocks, denounces, curses, weeps. He will not let them be at ease.

Worse by far, he insists it is in God's name that he concocts the bitter brew and stirs the fires.

◆ ◆ ◆

Now where are we? Where is Ezekiel?

Repeatedly our sense of time and place and sequence are jettisoned, warped; we are thrown off kilter in the world.

Are we in Jerusalem prior to the fall of the city? Are we amid the exiles? No clocks or maps at hand. We are both there and here, in the past and the awful present, at home, in exile.

And even in Babylon, it appears that the sin of the elders continues to fester.

Sin was the heaviest burden as the people were driven out.

And sin is rapidly imbedded in whatever tawdry social structure the deportees may put together, in the new and awful world of slavery.

◆ ◆ ◆

It is as though a criminal, convicted of crime and locked in prison, discovers among fellow prisoners ways and means of continuing larcenous, violent, self-serving conduct.

Conversion of heart? Prison and its equivalents, exile and slave labor, are extremely unlikely settings for such.

◆ ◆ ◆

Exile in this instance is both fact and metaphor.

Long before the Babylonian disaster, the prophets hammered away at the theme.

Jerusalem is a place of — exile. The community, apparently intact, laying claim to both temple and covenant, is spiritually exiled, at sea, alienated from God, from its own tradition and hope.

The people walk in darkness, amnesiacs in the world of the living. Generations, according to their own seers, have known and loved neither God nor one another.

Their worship is in effect a farce. From a temple far gone in moral decay, God was evicted.

Idols were installed in the holy place; idols that first had occupied their own hearts.

◆ ◆ ◆

At all cost Ezekiel must show and tell.

At all cost to a "sense of normalcy," bound as we are to the wheel of time and this world.

The God of Ezekiel is not so bound; and he would unbind the prophet.

Hence the bizarre, instantaneous visitations and transports. Ezekiel is plucked backward and forward in time and place, hither and yon, Jerusalem to Babylon, temple ritual to temple destroyed, the past made present, the present yielding to the past.

◆ ◆ ◆

In one scene, unparalleled in the Bible, God arises in distemper and fury. Like an Eastern potentate, proud, unforgivably insulted, he arises and abandons the temple.

He goes into exile — from those who have dared call themselves his own.

◆ ◆ ◆

And all this, be it understood, occurs in prospect and threat, prior to the fall of the holy city.

Ezekiel is privy to the future as well.

The chosen are to lose everything: possessions, land, temple. They will be driven out and out, beyond desert and mountains, like a herd of dumb cattle.

And so it transpires.

And now, do they imagine that in Babylon they have touched absolute bottom?

Be warned, worse is to come, Ezekiel thunders. Jerusalem will be utterly destroyed.

◆ ◆ ◆

The vision opens, the valley of bones.

It is as though the bones were souls, dead souls, all spirit having fled them. A multitude of the dead.

The fate of the exiles underlies the drama. They are not dead — and yet they are dead.

They have given up on life, on the future, on God.

◆ ◆ ◆

The valley of dry bones is an image on behalf of the wretched of the earth.

An image also on behalf of those who resist the creators of a wretched earth.

A foretaste of our gospel, and its word: he is God of the living, not of the dead. At the behest of the spirit of God, Ezekiel animates and urges the dead back to life.

Do not give up, you who have perished. Death abounds, yes, but life all the more so.

◆ ◆ ◆

The valley of dry bones is finally a scene of judgment. Those are summoned who make of the fields of life, a vast killing field.

Wreckers, destroyers of Hiroshima, Nagasaki, Vietnam, Grenada, Panama, Salvador, Nicaragua, Iraq, be warned. There is a God who witnesses, who stands with the victims.

As for yourselves, you stand under judgment.

THE TWO STICKS

Artful Ezekiel!

No sooner have the multitudes of the dead taken breath and stood erect than an oracle of purest hope is poured over them. It is like a balm of nard upon the brow of the dead, resurrecting their parched spirit.

It is as though the spirit had induced through all of creation (and in Yahweh!) a change of mood, as though the dark visage of life broke in a beatific smile, a smile of the Buddha.

◆ ◆ ◆

Away with defamation, judgment, thunderous bolts of recrimination! Here we have a totally different spirit, a tender heart, Yahweh the restorer, the conciliator whose gifts and grants are immemorially renewed.

◆ ◆ ◆

To Ezekiel: "Take a stick of wood in hand.
Scrawl on it a single word: Juda.
A second stick. Scrawl: Joseph.
As though the two were one,
join the sticks end to end.
Hold them before the people.
Thus the words
'Isolated,' 'Lonely' — are canceled.
That which was broken is restored.
For all at length are one.

"I tell you what shall be.
An absolute promise; this shall be.
And yet, and yet!
The ugly realities, the wretched present!
Hopeless, you cry. Bones, dry bones!" (37:15ff.)

◆ ◆ ◆

Nevertheless. Remote as it seems to a woeful present, something other than woe is possible. An event, an outcome you could no more attain of yourselves than that dead bones should assemble, stand erect, and walk.

◆ ◆ ◆

Let us speak of the present in detail, as those who look horror full in face — and yet are not turned to stone. "Idols...exile...crimes... abominations...infidelity..."

And then the promise: "restoration...your own land...one people ...loving obedience...covenant of peace...my dwelling with you..."

◆ ◆ ◆

Alas, the sticks of wood are broken, broken bones are everywhere. In Bosnia, in Somalia, the innocents die of starvation; in Iraq and Cuba, the war of sanctions rages strong. America and Europe are stalemated, stuck in self-interest and dread, bewildered as blind giants.

◆ ◆ ◆

We ask in torment of spirit: Is the promise here uttered and dramatized, meaningless, an illusion all the more cruel for being flatly, confidently, told of?

It must be said. Despite all, the vision, the drama of healing, unifying, resurrection — this continues, is verified, endures.

It stands for a strong hope, a sure promise. We lean upon it, live by it.

◆ ◆ ◆

More, we put the vision to the test.

Does the promise live?

It lives. In magnificent, awful, dangerous ways. In works never done with. And yet never abandoned.

An example comes to mind.

Sister Anne Montgomery, our dear friend of the Kairos Community in New York, together with Jim Reale and Fr. Steve Kelly and other friends from America and Europe, departed in the spring of '94, for former Yugoslavia.

They joined with others, Americans, Europeans, offering an alternative to the daily meed of death, working with orphans, in hospitals, offering food and shelter, bringing medical supplies, speaking to any who would listen of nonviolence and the concern and sorrow of friends across the world.

In the undertaking they were undoubtedly risking their lives. The "two sticks" of Ezekiel are hardly to be thought united; Bosnia and Herzegovina, "Loneliness" and "Isolation" — those two broken sticks symbolize well the tragic land. Two peoples could hardly be more broken, more desperately alienated one from the other.

An Italian who had led an earlier phase of the international team was shot and killed by a sniper.

◆ ◆ ◆

The American media? Indifferent or stalemated. They lap up violence like a pabulum, concentrate only on the horrifics of the war.

What can be done? What good can be achieved? At this point, no one can say; little light is available.

At least this can be claimed: that the peacemakers are offering an alternative, another — vision. Something other than the forces, so dark, so constantly and cruelly at work in a world of darkness.

GOG OF MAGOG, AND THE SPIRIT OF DEATH
Ezekiel 38–39

Having known in Jesus
"the loving kindness of our God,"
having known also
the "deceits of the devil
by which he seduces all nations,
which is to say
Gog and Magog" —

　　Secure in this knowledge
　　(though uneasy too),
　　　we take in account, hearing
　　the tremendous trump of judgment,
　　　"dies irae" of the nations.

　　Ezekiel
　　summons to judgment
　　　"Gog of Magog."

John of Revelation
　extends the indictment;
　　"All nations, which is to say,
　　　Gog and Magog."

　We are not to yield.
　"The deceits of the devil
　　by which he seduces all nations" —
　would persuade
　　that the indictment

excepts, exempts
a unique, virtuous,
noble entity —
To wit, this nation —
"horseman, pass by!"

No! the charge
unequivocal,
universal:
"all nations"
subject to judgment!

Therefore to Gog:
"I shall break the bow
in your left hand,
cast down the arrows
in your right hand."

Therefore,
"My people,
gather your weaponry
for firewood!
(enough for seven years!),
shields, bows, arrows,
spears, clubs."

And a loathsome
carrion feast follows:
nature reversed,
in plain daylight,
a nightmare;
birds, animals, summoned
to consume "a huge feast
of meat and blood,
the bodies of soldiers,
the blood of rulers of earth
killed like rams or goats,
lambs or fat bulls."

As also the angel of Revelation:
"To all the birds of midair:
Come to God's great feast!
Come eat the flesh of kings,
of generals and soldiers,

flesh of horses and riders,
flesh of all people,
slave, free, great and small!"
The cannibal feast —
it is "of God," declares Ezekiel,
    this anti-Eucharist
mocking the violent ones
who mickmock God.

    — the end,
    — the appalling form of the end.

It remains unclear —
What flame touched that tongue,
set it afire?
Exile, disorientation.
A multitude spun off its pivot.
And yet, and yet.
We know of one
among the harassed and ridiculed and broken —
who was not broken.
Whose vision led him on and on.
Led him back and forth.
To the edge of sanity. And back.
Led him back — to the future.

To Jerusalem,
to moral and religious and political renewal.
These events, he assures them
with the confident demeanor
of a madman or a mystic,
    "shall be." (38–39)

THE NEW TEMPLE, THE NEW COMMUNITY
Ezekiel 40–46

All to our benefit, we linger over the image of this man, an exile like the others, cast aside, a human debris — yet so unlike the others. A fearless organ of judgment.

We summon him to our side, the sole prophet known to have endured the harsh Babylonian years.

He voyages afar and returns, hither and yon, whether in the body or out of the body, we do not know. (He did not know.)

Babylon to Jerusalem, back and forth he hastens, for all the world like a levantine wizard on a flying carpet.

And the visions burst forth like the tail of that comet, bizarre and splendid and all but beyond human expression.

◆ ◆ ◆

Our Ezekiel — assailed as demented, analyzed like a cadaver on a couch by "experts," put down as tedious, curmudgeonly, calamity-ridden.

Dangerous, uncontainable he is!

Put him out the door, lock him up! Exclude him from the holy canon! Out of sight, out of mind!

We hear his sighs, his deep groans of spirit.

First the vision, then the consequence, his life in a gulag of "hard labor," his fidelity to the vision.

◆ ◆ ◆

Presently he undertakes the second portion of a task that must be thought thankless.

First came judgment.

Then the renewal of a disoriented, demoralized people.

◆ ◆ ◆

The exile was in effect a "life sentence."

It began with an inhuman roundup. A savage fate was meted out to all, a "collective punishment."

As usual, he meticulously notes the dates.

Today is the twenty-fifth year of exile, the fortieth since the destruction of the city and its temple. The year is 573 BCE, the first day of the fast preceding the Feast of Tents.

◆ ◆ ◆

After a generation of corvée, bafflement, misery — how initiate the task of restoration?

Another vision must be granted.

It is granted. A transport (in more senses than one!).

Ezekiel is rapt, like the unborn in a caul, in vision once more. Then he is transported bodily, as though sped along in the womb of mother God, toward the holy city.

◆ ◆ ◆

There, the miracle! It is as though the overgrowth and rubble of the holy temple were on the instant shaken, resurrected, the ruin reversed. As though the great squared stones, like the bones of the valley of defeat, leapt one upon on the other, alive, transfigured!

The temple, the temple!
Ezekiel is granted to see something which as yet has no existence —
pure and airy — and yet is sure to come, solid as the squared blocks of
a new city: the future.

◆ ◆ ◆

Measure, take the measure!
Measure of the future!
It is pure poetry,
everything is "as though, as though."
The vast awesome construction,
weightless, existing solely in anticipation,
as though in the palm of a cloudy hand —
stands there, sumptuous, pristine, complete.
The temple to be.
An entire structure, end to end,
foundation to summit,
massive, grandiose.
A temple built with angelic ease.
A new start.

◆ ◆ ◆

Which is to say, no mere building.
As the dry bones were scattered in a wilderness. Then resurrected,
rejuvenated. So with the temple.

◆ ◆ ◆

We can hardly conceive it: the wild hope that drives the prophet, on
and on, to the edge of time and this world.
Hope, and its firm grounding.
The temple.
Its foundation — the bedrock of the Promise.

◆ ◆ ◆

Now Ezekiel must rein in the visionary past.
All those mimes, those thunderous judgments, the confoundings and
confrontations!
They served their purpose.
The people have come home.
A new aeon!
Now he must act as draftsman, architect of the future.
Visionary yes — then visionary builder.

◆ ◆ ◆

The present task, its new imperatives.

He summons again those powers of his, powers of clairvoyance, of bilocation, evoking astonishing images of God, he an instrument resonating with God's word.

This for sake of the essentials, the blueprint.

◆ ◆ ◆

He must dispatch his soul (his soul must be sent) in an entirely new direction.

The future, make the future present; imagine new Jerusalem! Boldly he sets all in motion, stone upon stone.

◆ ◆ ◆

The task is no simple matter.

Laying out the dimensions and forms of a new building, however grand, must be understood as a symbol, a lead.

(In any case, as we know, despite the detailed blueprint traced by Ezekiel, the temple was never rebuilt. And that too is instructive as to larger meanings.)

One dares venture that the temple, qua construction, is all but beside the point.

◆ ◆ ◆

Concerning the remote past, the years of wine and roses, the years of high imperial culture, one thing is certain, as Yahweh insists.

Those years and their grandiosities are dead; the bones lie in the desert of exile, whence the people were set adrift.

The old temple worship, by turns blasé, meaningless, shameful, idolatrous, led only to ruin.

In question is the absolute need of a new "torah," covenant renewed, religious fervor, discipline, obedience, a politics of compassion, economic justice — the soul and body and heart of community, all reborn.

◆ ◆ ◆

The rebirth of the dry bones in the desert thus appears as a prelude and promise.

A new people: What will they look like?

Can such a people create and embody a human era, an alternative to the old culture of class, domination, death?

Amid much uncertainty, one element is sure.

The work is, must be, a work of God and a work of the people, both. Clumsy, but how else express it? An inter-section, a hyphenated enter-prise, a mutual-ity.

◆ ◆ ◆

Shall these bones live?

Of themselves they will never live; yet they must consent to live. The breath of the spirit must intervene and animate, again and again.

And for their part, the people, reduced as they are to a near nothing, must consent, welcome, breathe the spirit.

It is palpable, a kind of "daily bread." The hunger returns; the food is offered; we eat, or we die.

◆ ◆ ◆

What follows, especially in light of the stupendous visions that have gone before, strikes one as redundant, not to say wearying.

We had, from the start, the Ezekiel of contrasts: light and utmost darkness, the poetry sumptuous and elegant, then ferocious, calamitous.

◆ ◆ ◆

Now, through the remainder of the book, we are led — (and interminably) — through a maze rather than a vision.

An angel leads, an angel holding in hand a measuring rod.

In the space of four chapters, the angel meticulously takes the measure of the (hypothetical) temple.

Of the temple that never was.

◆ ◆ ◆

The scene resembles one of those *trompe l'oeil* architectural constructions that so tease the mind.

Such drawings lead one cunningly through three purported dimensions — while the drawing itself is, of course, in principle, two-dimensional! So the eye ends up where it started, a dead-end.

And the emotion, to be sure, teetering between amusement and annoyance.

◆ ◆ ◆

An anarchy of dreams?

We follow the angel's meticulous eye; it ranges over altar, doors, east gate, north gate, south gate, inner courtyards.

Then on to a cluster of buildings near the north gate, adjacent to the temple. The measure taken, of each and all.

These (sigh!) together with the initial instruction: "Tell the people of Israel of everything you see." And Ezekiel obeys — unto stupefaction.

The form, the future, hope, promise.

All of which, it is insisted, must first be imagined.

◆ ◆ ◆

The site invites a Visitor; more, a Resident. To be inspected, perhaps inhabited.

Thus, to borrow an image, a sound definition of poetry is verified. A real God enters the imaginary structure.

In an exact reversal of the stupendous, disconcerting exit of chapter 10, the glory of Yahweh once again takes up residence (44:4).

♦ ♦ ♦

This is the perennial boast of the temple priesthood (Solomon too gloried in the Real Presence [1 Kings 8:10–11]) — the Glory of God dwelling amid the believers.

♦ ♦ ♦

And this by way of anticipation and promise.

One day the Glory would be revealed in the midst of all people. Isaiah so spoke; the vocation of Israel was a prelude to the vocation of all.

Gentiles would come streaming to the temple from all the earth, to learn godly ways (2:3ff.). Micah struck the same theme (4:1–4).

♦ ♦ ♦

The early Christians seized on the tradition, to their own advantage.

According to Luke (1:22) the priest Zechariah receives a revelation, but is unable to confer the blessing on the people vigiling without. He doubts, and is struck dumb.

The revelation is given to another, Simeon, a devout and upright man. He is led by the Spirit to the temple; in the court he encounters and blesses the parents of the Newborn.

The One who is called by the angel of annunciation "holy" (Luke 1:35) has come to the holy place.

♦ ♦ ♦

The Infant is the Shekinah, the "Glory." The same Child is born as God's "salvation,...prepared in the presence of all peoples, a Light for revelation to the gentiles" as well as "glory to thy people Israel" (Luke 2:31, 32).

Law and Spirit, in a temple setting, have converged on Jesus.

♦ ♦ ♦

Meantime. Newly ensconced, the deity of Ezekiel (we have heard the voice before, and since) speaks up, stern and foreboding.

A strong implication: Yahweh is willing to close the scroll of memory as regards "idolatry, disgrace of my holy name." But only if...

♦ ♦ ♦

The measurement of the temple implies both a prelude and a question.

As to the future behavior of this recalcitrant people, the divine mood is watchful, hypothetical: "We shall see if..."

◆ ◆ ◆

Temple, new start. Construction, community.

Thus, by way of metaphor and inference, is implied the rebuilding of a people, a culture, a social entity capable of creating new political and economic forms.

The imagery is both dry and daring.

Dare we imagine?

God, God of the temple:

> Then [the angel] brought me...to the front of the temple. I looked, and behold, the glory of God filled the temple; and I fell upon my face. (44:4)

ALL, ALL MADE NEW
Ezekiel 47

God of the temple, God also of the sacred stream flowing from the temple:

> Eastward...it was ankle deep....Then the man led me through the water, and it was knee deep....Again he measured a thousand cubits, and led me through the water, and it was up to the loins....Again he measured,...and it was a river I could not pass through, for the water had risen. It was deep enough to swim in, a river that could not be passed through.
>
> And he said to me, "Human one, have you seen this?" (47:1–6)

And God of the multitudinous fish thriving in those waters:

> "Wherever the river goes, every living creature which swarms shall live, and there will be very many fish. For this water flows and cleanses, that even the waters of the sea may become fresh. ...Fisherfolk will stand beside the sea....From the borders of the dead sea to the north, there will be place for the spreading of nets....Its fish will be of very many kinds, like the fish of the Mediterranean itself." (47:9–10)

And God of "the variety of trees, and their fruits" that grow beside the waters:

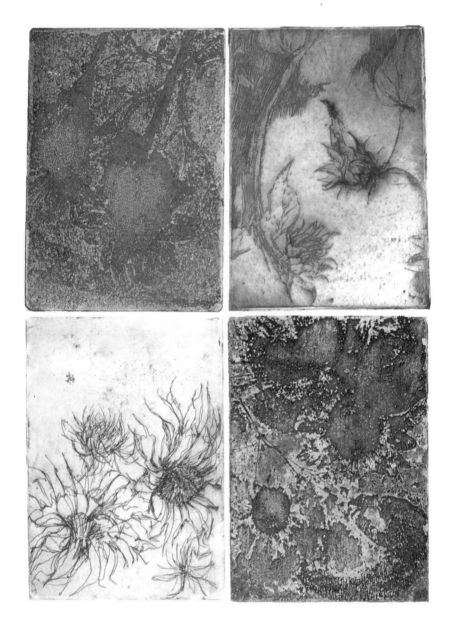

"Their leaves will not wither, nor their fruit fail, but they will bear fresh fruit every month, because the water flows from the sanctuary. Their fruit will be for food, and their leaves for healing." (47:12)

◆ ◆ ◆

Delightful, instructive. Flowing from the temple-to-be-imagined, beneath the sanctuary, a river (imagined too) takes its start, as though struck from rock by the rod of Aaron.

Its waters are sparse. Then mysteriously they mount and mount: to a flood, impassable.

And the fecundity, the splendor, pure poetry!

It is as though the image of the temple surpassed every possibility allowed a mere structure; it bursts its walls, it lives!

It becomes in the prophet's vision a source, center, matrix, avatar of God.

◆ ◆ ◆

The evangelist John is enchanted with the imagery, and borrows it whole cloth for conclusion of his Revelation:

Then he showed me the river of the water of life, bright as crystal, flowing from the throne of God and of the Lamb through the middle of the street of the city. Also on either side of the river, the tree of life with its twelve kinds of fruit, yielding its fruit each month. And the leaves of the tree were for the healing of the nations. (22:1–2)

ALL MANNER OF THINGS SHALL BE WELL!
Ezekiel 49

And the name of the city shall henceforth be, "The Lord is here." (49:35)

Perhaps the assonance of "Yahve-sham" recalls "Jerusalem."

But more, how much more! Here, reduced to a name, a phrase, "the roll, the rise, the carol, the creation."

The scroll of Ezekiel, the unutterable suffering, the hope that beats on. The Promise.

Thank you, good brother and friend.